MAINE
Off the Beaten Path

MAINE

Off the Beaten Path™

by

Wayne Curtis

A Voyager Book

The Globe Pequot Press

Old Saybrook, Connecticut

Cover illustration of Portland Head Light by Cathy Johnson
Text illustrations by Carole Drong

Off the Beaten Path is a registered trademark of The Globe Pequot Press, Inc.

Library of Congress Cataloging-in-Publication Data

Curtis, Wayne, 1957–
  Maine—off the beaten path / by Wayne Curtis. — 1st ed.
    p.   cm.
  "A Voyager book."
  Includes index.
  ISBN 1-56440-022-0
  1. Maine—Guidebooks.   I. Title.
  F17.3.C87   1992
  917.4104'43—dc20   92-7124
                                                      CIP

Manufactured in the United States of America
First Edition/Second Printing

To Susanne and Caleb

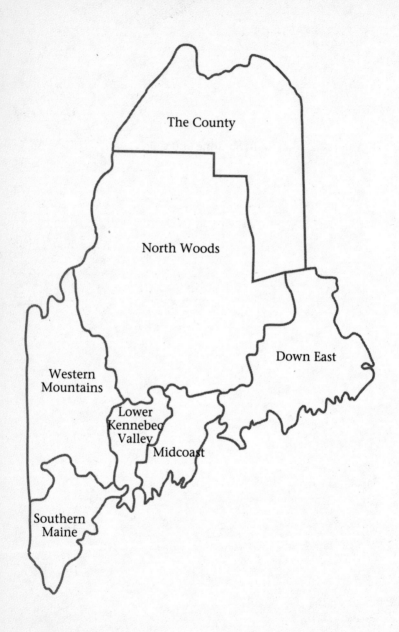

The County

North Woods

Western
Mountains

Down East

Lower
Kennebec
Valley

Midcoast

Southern
Maine

Contents

Acknowledgments

As with any guide covering an area as large as Maine, a number of people helped with tips, advice, and encouragement. Among those deserving thanks: Dale Kuhnert, Janice Brand, and Monte Paulsen for giving me a license to write articles about the state, as well as Louise Klaila, Beth Crichlow, Chris and Ted Sprague, Cynthia Hacinli, Tom Thomsen, Pat Rossi, Karen Stimpson, and the many employees at the various attractions around the state. Special thanks go to the Maine State Historic Preservation Commission and the Maine Office of Tourism, both of whom provided the photographs used in rendering the illustrations in this guide.

Introduction

An acquaintance from Boston drove up to Maine one weekend a while back looking for some of that remote, storm-tossed coast he had heard about. He crossed the bridge at Kittery, got off the interstate, and headed resolutely up Route 1. After a couple of hours of driving, he decided that Maine, in fact, looked a lot like suburban Boston. The rugged coast and small villages, he concluded, were figments of an effective if misleading advertising campaign. He turned around and went home, rather pleased with himself for having deflated a pernicious myth.

Seeing Maine takes a bit more creativity and persistence than that. Route 1 is to Maine what McDonald's is to Paris: an interloper that's peculiarly alluring to visitors. To find the real Maine, you need to wander farther afield, getting off the primary arteries to explore the winding back roads. And even that is sometimes not enough. Every so often you'll need to trade your car for canoe, windjammer, or hiking boots to find the Maine that looms so large in the popular imagination.

And that Maine does exist. You can still find unspoiled coastal villages without a tee-shirt or ice-cream shop. And lakeside campsites along pristine lakes deep in the spruce and fir forest. And intriguing small museums where you're the only visitor present, allowing for undistracted browsing. In your travels you'll also discover that there's little in the way of extravagance or outlandishness—no Elvis museums, nor much in the way of garish architecture. Even the twenty-bedroom summer "cottages" dating from the turn of the century seem understated and subdued. The most alluring attractions in the state reflect its flinty New England roots: a sweep of unadorned coastline; a magnificently simple Federal-era house; an undisturbed five-acre pond accessible only by foot.

The state is often divided into two regions: the Coast and the North Woods. But that view simplifies things a bit much. For one, few coastal areas often bear much resemblance to one another. Other than the frosty waters that wash their shores, the sandy beaches of York County have little in common with the bold headlands near Cutler or with the oceanside farms along the midcoast. The same applies to the North Woods. The generally flat terrain found on the popular canoe route down the Allagash River is reminiscent of Minnesota, with the horizon defined by the sharp spires of spruce trees at water's edge. In contrast, brawny and broad Carrabassett Valley seems to have more in common with Montana, featuring distant, open views of rounded, rocky mountains. And then there are the vast, rolling farmlands of Aroostook County, which curtly defeat all attempts to categorize Maine. For those willing to wander off the main track, Maine's breadth and diversity rarely fail to impress.

Exploring backroad Maine requires a degree of conviction. The beaten path is more deeply rutted here than in many states. Tourism generates some $2 billion a year; it's the second largest industry after timber. And because travel services tend to congregate near the more popular destinations, the traveler's route becomes entrenched and reinforced. Parts of Route 1 offer the best example, but you'll come across others, such as the commercial strip leading to Bar Harbor and Acadia National Park. Maine's beaten path isn't that much different from suburban Boston. Just remember that these places serve an important function: They help concentrate less-enterprising visitors in a few places, leaving the rest of the state open for quiet exploration.

Before you set off exploring the state's secondary road network, be aware that it was not created with tourism in mind. At times, it seems not to have been created with transportation in mind. Why else would they put all those roads down dead-end peninsulas along the coast and erect barricades across perfectly serviceable gravel thoroughfares in the North Woods? The old Maine chestnut ending with the kicker "You can't get there from here" didn't germinate in a fertile imagination. It had a solid basis in reality. Those who do best in their endeavor of investigating backroad Maine's less-traveled byways tend to be well endowed with patience and possessed of a finely honed sense of adventure.

They also tend to have a copy of *DeLorme's Maine Atlas and Gazetteer*. First published in 1976, the atlas breaks the state down into some seventy road atlas–sized maps. If cut out and assembled, DeLorme's map of the state would measure some 8 by 12 feet, providing more than enough detail on backroads and byways, right down to dirt lanes that peter out into jeep tracks and foot trails. Updated annually, the atlas is essential for anyone intent on getting seriously off the main track. It's available for $11.95 at many Maine stores as well as at DeLorme's Map Store in Freeport. For more information, call the publisher at 865–4171.

Another useful publication is free, published by the Maine Publicity Bureau. *Maine Invites You* is available at many tourist information booths, but often you must ask for it. This thick guide—nearly 300 pages long—consists primarily of page after page of advertisements for restaurants and hotels. The most valuable section will be found in the back: a town-by-town listing of inns and hotels with their addresses and phone numbers. You're likely to find this directory remarkably handy at some point in your travels. With these two publications and *Maine: Off the Beaten Path,* you'll be fully outfitted for a proper Maine adventure.

Even with these tools in hand, be prepared for some geographic surprises. Maine is fairly massive by New England standards. The geographic center of the state is near Katahdin Iron Works, deep in the North Woods and a long, long drive from the South Coast. Travelers often charge into the state from New Hampshire and fail to notice that the map scale has changed; an inch, which earlier covered 10 miles, now covers 20. They become puzzled why it suddenly takes so long to get everywhere. When planning a trip to the northern part of the state, keep one fact in mind: Portland is closer to Manhattan than it is to Madawaska.

There's also the issue of access. Maine has one of the smallest percentages of publicly owned land in the country. Much of the dramatic coastline featured on wall calendars and place mats is privately owned. Nice to look at, but if you try to visit you'll be cited for trespassing. As a result, those few coastal areas that are publicly owned—such as Acadia National Park—tend to be overrun. One way to circumvent this is to view the coast from the water, where private property and trespass is less of an issue. In addition, the state owns and maintains literally hundreds of islands that are open to public use. Windjammer trips, naturalist expeditions, and sea kayak tours all offer a means to visit these salty wildernesses, even if you don't have your own oceangoing vessel.

The North Woods are also privately owned for the most part, but access is less of an issue. Timber companies own much of the woodlands in inland Washington County and from Rangeley Lake northward to Fort Kent. They maintain an extensive network of logging roads for their daily operations, but most are happy to share the roads with the public. Some are open without charge. Others, particularly those managed by North Maine Woods Inc. in the northwestern part of the state, are tightly controlled through a network of gatehouses. Daily and overnight fees are levied much as they are at national parks. Logging roads and gatehouses are all detailed in DeLorme's atlas.

Some of the most distinctive private lands in the state are owned and managed by the Maine chapter of the Nature Conservancy. I've included several Nature Conservancy properties in this guide and simply can't say enough favorable things about the organization. Since its founding in 1956 (naturalist Rachel Carson was among the nine organizers), the Conservancy has acquired more than 60,000 acres of Maine, from dramatic islands far offshore to untouched inland lakes and their feeder streams. Conservancy holdings are managed primarily for wildlife, but the public is invited to visit many of these preserves during daylight hours. (Overnight camping is prohibited, and groups of twelve or more must have advance permission.) I encourage all readers to support the Conservancy's efforts to preserve the state's natural heritage by becoming members ($15 for individuals; $25 for a family). The Conservancy also publishes a helpful guide to the more than sixty preserves it currently manages. Write: The Nature Conservancy, 122 Main Street, Topsham, ME 04086.

What's the best season to travel? "Summer" is often used as a verb in Maine, and the state naturally tends to be more crowded during the summer season, when the weather is most reliable. By coming at another time, you can avoid the crowds and have the place more to yourself. June is an agreeable month to visit Maine's towns and cities, but those with outdoor inclinations will likely find themselves fighting a losing battle against black flies and mosquitos. The weather and insects tend to be most cooperative in September and early October, when the landscape is at its most spectacular. These advantages don't come without a cost: Many of the state's smaller museums and other attractions are closed for the season by then.

Visiting in winter also has its benefits. Off-season rates apply throughout much of the state (except near ski areas, of course). Summer tourist destinations, such as Boothbay Harbor and Old Orchard Beach, take on a melancholy and shuttered look; but the rest of the state displays a local vigor often not visible during the warmer seasons. Greenville becomes a snowmobilers' mecca, a fueling stop for those exploring the state's 3,000-mile snowmobile trail network. Portland's arts and theater season is in full swing. And even Acadia attracts hundreds of visitors who've found John D. Rockefeller's carriage roads an ideal cross-country skiing destination.

No matter when you visit, take the time to enjoy the state fully. The more narrowly you target your sights, and the more relaxed a pace you set, the better your chances of discovering Maine. Learn from long-time visitors to the state, who often return annually to a favorite inn or cabin. Find a base and use it to launch unhurried forays into the countryside. Sit for a day or two in a rocking chair with a view of the coast, and slowly the landscape will start to come alive. You'll begin to notice the patterns in the granite and the lichens on the rocks. Soon you'll start recognizing the lobster-men working offshore. The sounds of the distant foghorns will take on a familiar, comfortable tone. Just sitting and watching may be the best way to visit a state that begrudges giving up its best secrets.

The area code for the entire state is 207. All prices are current as of autumn 1991. As usual, expect moderate increases. This applies particularly to state-run facilities, including state parks. Because of state budget problems, hours are being cut back and user fees are rising. Some destinations that were once free are now charging admission. To avoid disappointment, it's best to call ahead to confirm times and costs.

Off the Beaten Path in Southern Maine

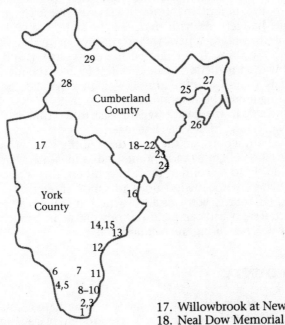

29

28

Cumberland
County

27
25
26

17   18–22
23
24

York
County

16

14,15
13

12

6   7   11
4,5
8–10
2,3
1

1. Naval Shipyard Museum
2. Fort McClary
3. Fort Foster
4. Vaughan Woods Memorial
5. Hamilton House
6. Sarah Orne Jewett House
7. Mount Agamenticus
8. Old York Historical Society
9. Wiggly Bridge
10. Cliff Walk
11. Marginal Way
12. Laudholm Farm
13. White Columns
14. Tom's of Maine
15. Seashore Trolley Museum
16. Ocean Park

17. Willowbrook at Newfield
18. Neal Dow Memorial
19. Morse-Libby House
20. Wadsworth-Longfellow
    House
21. Portland Observatory
22. Lightship *Nantucket*
23. Spring Point Museum
24. Museum at Portland
    Head Light
25. Wolfe's Neck Farm
26. Eagle Island
27. Peary-MacMillan Arctic
    Museum
28. Jones Museum of Glass and
    Ceramics
29. Sabbathday Lake Shaker
    Community

SOUTHERN MAINE

You could look for a greater range of terrain and regional character than you'll find in southern Maine, but there's not much point in it. The region boasts everything from small coastal harbors to gentle, wooded mountains; from the state's largest city to quiet backwoods hamlets. As with much of the state, the bulk of the population lives along a narrow crescent near the coast. This area was where the ships first deposited the early settlers, and where later highway construction made it easiest to live. The main arteries—such as Route 1 and the turnpike—tend to parallel the shoreline, creating a broad transportation corridor with links to Boston and southward. In contrast, traveling east to west (or vice versa) presents something more of a challenge.

Historical attractions are the chief draw of the southern region, and those who delight in early homesteads and cluttered antiques stores are likely to be content here. In addition, this is also beach territory, where you can find miles of sandy shorefront to walk and relax. Of course, you can also swim, but it helps if you're a hardy sort: The ocean temperature tops out at not much more than sixty degrees during the balmiest of days.

YORK COUNTY

A reasonable argument could be made to eliminate coastal York County entirely from this guide. There are few places here that haven't been discovered by tourists, and few places that haven't discovered tourists and oriented themselves to the trade. In fact, a few years ago the *Maine Times* proposed, presumably in jest, that the state should just give York County to New Hampshire, which would in exchange allow Mainers toll-free travel on its turnpike. Maine never acted on this unsolicited advice, but the idea does point up the popular notion that York County has been engulfed by the megalopolis spreading northward from Boston.

This persistent conception notwithstanding, you're likely to find that York County still has plenty to offer, particularly if you take pains to avoid Route 1. The county has a strong historical tradition with roots in the seventeenth and eighteenth centuries, and many of its attractions reflect this early history. And perhaps surprisingly, the inland townships contain inviting

2

hardwood forests as peaceful and remote as you'll find anywhere in the state.

Kittery and Vicinity

Your first encounter with Maine is likely to be at Kittery, which lies just over the I-95 bridge from Portsmouth, N.H. A growing number of factory outlets cluster along both sides of Route 1, creating a sort of Scylla and Charybdis of consumer culture. Venture here at your own risk.

In contrast, Kittery's small downtown has a sleepy, backyard feel, as if it had been overlooked by both travelers and the years. Dominating the town is the venerable Portsmouth Naval Shipyard. This, the navy's first yard, was established on Dennett's Island in 1806, then expanded to neighboring Seavey Island in 1866. The main entrance is in the middle of Kittery, just beyond the Rice Library, a fine manse of elaborate Victorian brickwork. On the base is the **Naval Shipyard Museum,** which traces the history of the yard. In an immense room in the former enlisted men's barracks you'll find ship models and naval artifacts from the nineteenth century, including uniforms, shipbuilding tools, and memorabilia from past launchings.

Perhaps the most interesting exhibits focus on the current century, reflecting the yard's current central mission of overhauling and rebuilding submarines. Ten large-scale submarine models (up to 6 feet long) are on display, tracing the evolution of the submarine from early concept to advanced seagoing vessel. Other submarine-related items include artifacts recovered from German submarines that surrendered during World War II. The museum is currently open year-round by appointment only but may begin limited regular hours in 1992. Call for more information: 438–3550.

Continuing in a military vein, a pair of historic coastal forts on the Maine side of Portsmouth Harbor invite exploration as you continue along Route 103. **Fort McClary** has gone through a number of permutations and additions since this bluff was first fortified in 1715. The original fort was expanded and strengthened during the American Revolution, the War of 1812, the Civil War, and then again during the 1898 Spanish-American War. The most prominent building on the site—located amid a labyrinth of earthworks—is a handsome hexagonal wooden blockhouse atop a fieldstone and granite foundation. Built in 1844, it has the distinction of being the last blockhouse constructed in the state. The blockhouse and site are now administered as a state memorial and are open daily except Wednesdays 10:00 A.M. to 5:00 P.M.

The remains of **Fort Foster** on nearby Gerrish Island (visible from Fort McClary) are of more contemporary vintage. This early fort was expanded during World War II, when it was used to anchor one end of a massive net stretched across Portsmouth Harbor to keep inquisitive German submarines from prowling around the naval yard. The ninety-acre site, now operated as a park by the town of Kittery, is dotted with hulking concrete walls and towers. Attractive pebbly beaches are set aside for various activities, including scuba diving, windsurfing, and swimming, and a long pier is open to fishing. Picnic tables and sweeping lawns provide dramatic views of lighthouses and an old offshore Coast Guard station, lending the whole area a fine sense of Gothic melodrama.

The park is on the southern tip of Gerrish Island, accessible from the mainland over a small bridge. Look for the sign to Gerrish Island on Route 103 just north of Kittery Point village, then make the first right over the bridge. The park is open daily 10:00 A.M. to 8:00 P.M. Admission is $1 for adults and 50 cents for children, plus $2 per vehicle.

Salmon Falls River Valley

Some travelers become so smitten with the coast that they overlook the inland areas. Don't make the same mistake. **Vaughan Woods Memorial,** a 250-acre park 12 miles inland, provides welcome solace from the relative crowding and congestion along the coast. The park is located on a quiet, unspoiled stretch of the Salmon Falls River near South Berwick. Picnic tables are spread about a quiet pine grove near the parking area. You can wander the trails down a gentle hill through hemlocks and maples to Cow Cove, where the first cattle in Maine were landed off a ship from Denmark in 1634. (Maine's first permanent settlement was just upstream.) From a riverside bench, take the time to enjoy the picture-perfect view across the cove of what is arguably Maine's most outstanding example of Georgian architecture.

That splendid manor home, called **Hamilton House,** is open to the public but isn't accessible from along the shore. Return to your car and take the first left on Vaughan Lane, then drive to the end and park in the field. Built in 1787 by Colonel Jonathan Hamilton, a successful West Indies trader and merchant from Portsmouth, the house passed through various hands before it was eventually acquired by the Society for the Preservation of New England Antiquities in 1949. With its regal aspect, wonderful proportions, and picturesque setting, the house will impress even those notably uninterested in either architecture or history. The grounds are immaculately maintained and feature a hedge-enclosed garden complete with sundial and unobtrusive bits of classical statuary here and there. Guided tours of the house, offered throughout the summer, reveal a fine collection of Chippendale and Sheraton furniture.

To reach Vaughan Woods and the Hamilton House, turn onto Route 101 (toward New Hampshire) from Route 236, then make an immediate right. Vaughan Woods is 2.7 miles on the left. The park is open daily except Wednesdays 10:00 A.M. to 5:00 P.M. Hamilton House is open July 1 to October 15 on Tuesdays, Thursdays, and weekends noon to 5:00 P.M. A guided tour costs $2. For more information call 384-5269.

In the town of South Berwick, stop at the **Sarah Orne Jewett House,** which presides over the main intersection in the middle of town. Jewett died in 1909; she is widely regarded as one of Maine's best writers and has seen her stature rise in academia in recent years. Indeed, novelist Willa Cather once wrote that Jewett's *Country of the Pointed Firs* would take its place alongside Mark Twain's *Huckleberry Finn* and Nathaniel Hawthorne's *Scarlet Letter* on the shelf of great American literature. *Country of the Pointed Firs,* a collection of tales of Maine coastal life (Jewett summered in Martinsville in Knox County), remains in print and is available in paperback in many Maine bookstores. Jewett also wrote the novel (now out of print) *The Tory Lover,* which was set at nearby Hamilton House.

The Jewett House, built in 1774, has been fully restored and furnished to reflect the period when the author lived and worked, 1849–1909. It features exceptional detailing, including early wood paneling and some of the original eighteenth-century wallpaper. Like the Hamilton House, the Jewett house is owned by the Society for the Preservation of New England Antiquities, and SPNEA offers tours during the summer. The house is at 101 Portland Street and is open June 1 to October 15 on Tuesdays, Thursdays, and weekends noon to 5:00 P.M. A guided tour costs $2. For more information, call 384–5269.

Be sure to visit also the Eastman-Jewett House next door, better known these days as the South Berwick Public Library. Except for the addition of dozens of freestanding bookcases, the house appears largely unchanged from earlier days. A fire lies kindled in the fireplace, a pendulum clock marks time on the wall, and several rooms have been papered with wallpaper designed after traditional nineteenth-century woodblock prints.

To get your bearings en route back to the coast, consider a detour to the top of **Mount Agamenticus,** a 692-foot hill that may be climbed by foot or ascended by car. Long a navigational landmark for sailors, Agamenticus has a diverse and intriguing history. Aspinquid, a revered Pawtucket Indian who died at the age of ninety-four in 1692, was said to be buried on this mound in a funeral ceremony that involved the sacrifice of more than 6,000 animals. In recent years, the hill has served less sanguinary and more prosaic functions as a ski area and a site for radio towers. With the communications stations, the parking lot, and the defunct ski lodge, the summit is a bit cluttered for purists. Never mind that. Scramble up the fire tower here and you can enjoy spectacular views westward toward New Hampshire's White Mountains and eastward along the coast from Cape Ann in Massachusetts well up Maine's convoluted shoreline. The summit road is accessible off Agamenticus Road.

The Yorks

Return to the coast and you'll find yourself amid the Yorks. Although there's technically only one York, three areas have maintained distinct identities and separate names: York Village, York Harbor, and York Beach. And as travelers soon discover, each town has its own particular personality.

Historians flock to York Village, where they find one of the finest collections of historic buildings open to the public in the state of Maine. First settled around 1630, York Village is a peaceful town of tree-lined streets, with few intrusions from the modern age. The **Old York Historical Society** maintains seven historic buildings scattered between York River and York Street, and each has a distinct flavor and intriguing past. Visitors set their own pace in exploring local history hereabouts, wandering by foot or by car from one building to the next or taking a break for rubbings of the early tombstones at the Old Burying Ground.

Among the buildings open to the public are the Old Gaol, built in 1719 to house both debtors and hardened criminals. Constructed of fieldstone walls more than 2 feet thick, the jail, which was in use until 1860, is considered the oldest public building in the United States. The building has been a museum since 1900, and today the cells, dungeon, and gaoler's quarters are furnished as they might have been around 1790.

Other historic York buildings include Jefferds Tavern, a public house dating from 1759, and the nearby Old Schoolhouse, with its furnishings circa 1745. Along the York River you'll find the John Hancock warehouse and wharf, once owned by the famous signer of the Declaration of Independence. In the words of one historian, Hancock was "more successful in politics than in business." This wharf, restored in 1950 after a long and lackluster history, is York's only commercial building.

The Old York buildings are open mid-June through September and on Columbus Day weekend, Tuesday through Sunday 10:00 A.M. to 4:00 P.M. One ticket provides admission to all buildings. Tickets are available at Jefferds Tavern, on Lindsay Road across from the imposing First Parish Congregational Church. Adults are $6.00, children $2.50. For more information, call 363–4974.

Just downstream from York Village (or a short drive on Route 1A), you'll come to York Harbor, as gracious and sophisticated as York Village but with a slightly more modern flair in its architecture and tone. Take a break from history and stretch your legs along the waterfront walking path. If you head south on Route 103, you'll soon see on your right **Wiggly Bridge,** said to be the smallest suspension bridge in the world. Park along the road and follow the path across this unique footbridge (learning how it got its name in the process) to enjoy a quiet walk through the woods on the far bank. The trail loops back along Barrel Mill Pond; or more ambitious hikers may continue on, walking on dirt roads to Lindsay Road near Hancock Wharf in York Village.

Heading along the path the other way will take you along York Harbor's waterfront to Harbor Beach, where the modern and pricey Stage Neck Inn occupies a prominent bluff overlooking the harbor's mouth. The path is narrow and quiet, a world removed from the present day. If your appetite demands more historic buildings, visit the Sayward-Wheeler House, owned by the Society for the Preservation of New England Antiquities. This fine merchant's home was built in the 1760s and offers a grand view of the harbor. Inside, look for the chinaware Captain Jonathan Sayward hauled back from a successful 1745 battle against the French at Louisbourg. The mansion's well-maintained grounds are the first you cross when you head eastward on the path from Route 103. The building is also accessible from Barrel Lane. Open June 1 to October 15 on Tuesdays, Thursdays, and weekends noon to 5:00 P.M. A guided tour costs $2.

If you're enjoying the walking so far, continue past Harbor Beach to the **Cliff Walk,** a dramatic shoreline trail that hugs rocky crags and provides excellent views of the harsh coastline as well as of some of the splendid nineteenth-century summer homes along the way. The trail crosses private land but is open to the public within certain limitations (e.g., no radio playing, picnicking, or bus tours). The trail, which may be rough going for those with unsure footing, also provides access to several small, pebbly beaches. The trail begins at the end of Harbor Beach Road, and you'll find limited parking there.

Northward up the coast, York Beach has a more laid-back feeling than its brethren. The pleasant seaside town draws its history more from the late nineteenth century than from the colonial era, and it is decidedly more raucous and less polished. A popular turn-of-the-century destination for urban dwellers seeking to elude the summer heat, York Beach still retains a mild honky-tonk flavor, one that has been considerably tempered by recent gentrification. Short Sands Beach fronts the town and offers ocean swimming (there's a metered parking lot adjacent to the beach); and the usual shorefront amusements—the Fun-O-Rama arcade, palm readers, and candlepin bowling—offer pleasant diversions for sunburnt or restless beachgoers.

Ogunquit Area

North of York Beach is Ogunquit, a pleasant seaside town that was "discovered" by artists such as Edward Hopper and Maurice Prendergast, who in turn attracted the gentry. That now-familiar process began over a century ago, but Ogunquit still retains its artistic flavor (galleries abound) and remains an exceedingly popular seaside destination. The town fairly brims with motels, restaurants, souvenir shops, and self-styled "resorts," but to its credit it has managed to retain the character of a more restful era.

The best way to enjoy Ogunquit is to park your car and leave it for the duration, spending your time traveling by foot. And the best way to see the sea is along **Marginal Way,** a winding footpath donated to the town in 1923 by a farmer who used the route to usher cattle to summer pasture. Today, strollers, sunbathers, and hikers are far more common than cows. Parking for the trail may be found near the town police station on Cottage Street. More ambitious walkers could make a day of it by parking further up the coast at Footbridge Beach (turn off Route 1 on Ocean Street). From there, ramble your way along the water's sandy edge southward for about a mile to the main beach. Cross the bridge on Beach Street into the center of Ogunquit for lunch at any of the town's many eateries, then resume your walk after lunch.

Pick up the main pathway across from Seacastles Resort on Shore Road. The route meanders away from the sandy strand and along the twisting, rocky shoreline for the next mile and a quarter, with benches well placed for reading, relaxing, or restfully contemplating the surf. In places you'll find yourself surrounded by wild roses or beneath a delicate canopy of cedar trees. Take the time to scramble down to the shore's edge, where you can explore tide pools and the rugged coastal geology.

The pathway ends at Perkins Cove, a picturesque and well-protected harbor clotted with fishing boats and pleasure craft. The cove is a popular tourist destination and boasts more than its fair share of jewelry stores, crafts shops, and restaurants. Parking is a perpetual problem in summer. (Something not afflicting those arriving by foot.) Be sure to investigate the pedestrian footbridge that crosses the harbor's entrance. When a tall-masted sailboat needs to enter or depart, it blasts its horn and whoever happens to be handy raises the narrow bridge by pressing a series of buttons.

To return to your car, board one of the trolley buses that stop frequently at Perkins Cove. These modern gas-powered trolleys are operated as a nonprofit venture by the chamber of commerce and feature detailing of brass, oak, and leather. The fare is 50 cents, which you deposit in the wooden box next to the driver. The trolleys run through the center of Ogunquit and as far as Footbridge

Beach, with many stops in between. Between July 1 and Labor Day the trolley operates between 8:00 A.M. and 11:00 P.M. During the "shoulder" seasons, starting in late May and extending through Columbus Day, the trolley operates until 9:00 P.M.

North of Ogunquit you'll find the Wells National Estuarine Research Reserve, a coastal wildlife refuge still in the process of being cobbled together. Assembled through local private initiative, the reserve's thousands of acres of coastal marsh and forested uplands are managed as a wildlife sanctuary and for scientific research. The reserve includes 1,600 acres of privately owned land at Laudholm Farm, 4,000 acres of federal land managed as the Rachel Carson National Wildlife Refuge, and additional acreage that will someday emerge as Laudholm State Park but as yet remains undeveloped.

Laudholm Farm provides the setting for a beguiling walk through both complex ecosystems and a long-gone era. Once maintained as a summer residence by George C. Lord, a prominent New England railroad tycoon, this historic saltwater farm is now owned by the Laudholm Trust, which acquired the land in 1986 with donations from nearly 2,500 people. The trust manages the property, maintains research facilities, and offers a variety of naturalist programs for students and the public alike. The centerpiece of the property is a majestic Victorian farmhouse with graceful barns and outbuildings. The farm complex perches on a gentle rise amid open fields, providing views down the coast toward Ogunquit. Nature guides and trail maps are available in the visitor center in the farmhouse.

The farm offers 7 miles of trails for wandering through fields, forest, and along boardwalks through coastal wetlands. You might even take a swim at the quiet barrier beach, a 0.75-mile walk through meadow and forest and past several summer homes. Pick up an interpretive pamphlet for the Knight Trail, a fine introduction to the local habitat. Birdwatchers will be delighted in the mix of terrain hereabouts: Some 250 species have been observed within the reserve itself. If you're without a clue about the flora and fauna you're looking at, sign up for one of the guided naturalist tours offered throughout the year.

In July and August, parking at the trust is $5 per car; the remainder of the year parking is free. There is no charge to enter the grounds, which are open 8:00 A.M. to 5:00 P.M. daily. The visitor center is open Monday through Saturday 10:00 A.M. to 4:00

P.M., and Sundays noon to 4:00 P.M. To reach Laudholm Farm, turn right off Route 1 on Laudholm Farm Road at the blinking light just north of Harding Books. Turn left at fork and then make the next right into the farm's entrance. For more information call 646–1555.

Just north of Laudholm Farm is the headquarters of the Rachel Carson National Wildlife Refuge, named after the crusading biologist and author, who spent many of her summers in Maine exploring the tidal waters. Carson also worked for the wildlife service throughout her career. The refuge consists of nine parcels along the southern coast (when acquisitions are complete, more than seven thousand acres will be protected), but very little of it has been developed for visitors.

At the refuge headquarters, however, you'll find a mile-long nature trail offering a good introduction to the salt marsh ecosystem. The Carson Trail skirts the edge of a fine marsh, with informative educational stations along the way. Stop at the main kiosk near the parking area and pick up a free trail map and brochure. The refuge headquarters is open from dawn to dusk throughout the year. The trail is located on Route 9 just off Route 1. For more information call refuge headquarters at 646–9226.

The Kennebunks

Kennebunkport, a slumbering seaside town long known for its elegant accommodations, found itself thrust into the national spotlight when George Bush was elected president in 1988. Bush, whose family has summered in Kennebunkport for decades, often visits at the house built by his grandfather at Walker Point, a dramatic peninsula jutting out into the Gulf of Maine. Needless to say, Bush's rise to the presidency led to some changes in town, foremost among them an increase in tourist traffic. Parking is frequently problematic near Dock Square in the center of town, but spaces seem to be available on side streets at some distance from the center.

On Main Street looking down toward Dock Square is **White Columns,** more formally known as the Richard A. Nott Memorial. This impressive home, constructed in 1853, will please anyone interested in America during the Victorian era. When Elizabeth Nott gave the house to the local historical society in

1983, it was with the proviso that nothing be changed. Her stipulation was actually a continuation of a policy her family maintained for years. The place still boasts the original wallpaper, carpeting, and furnishings, creating a virtual time capsule of Victorian life. Guided tours are offered from mid-June to mid-October between 1:00 and 4:00 P.M. Wednesdays, Thursdays, and Fridays. On Fridays tea is served in the barn and gift shop behind the house. The tour is $2; tea and tour is $3.

The handsome inland town of Kennebunk, located 3.5 miles from the port on Routes 35 and 9A, offers a slower pace and less of a seasonal ebb and flow. Between the port and the town, on Summer Street, you'll pass through the Kennebunk Historic District with its fine examples of grand nineteenth-century architecture. Be sure to note the "wedding cake house," a flamboyant building that resembles, well . . . a wedding cake. The story is that a local sea captain rushed to sea before a proper cake could be baked for his new bride. This ornate brick house, which he had built upon his return, was his way of making amends. You'll know which one it is when you pass by.

The Brick Store Museum, located at 117 Main Street, was founded in 1936 by Edith Cleaves Barry on the second floor of an 1825 brick store. The modest museum showcasing local history has since expanded down the block and now includes the adjacent three buildings. Despite its growth the place remains quite intimate and personal. Three or four special historical exhibits are presented each year in the first-floor galleries. Permanent collections are housed on the second floor and include maritime paintings, ship models, and early nineteenth-century portraits and furnishings. The museum is open year-round Tuesdays through Fridays 10:00 A.M. to 4:30 P.M., and from April 15 to December 15 on Saturdays 10:00 A.M. to 4:30 P.M. Admission is $2 for adults and $1 for children. For more information call 985–4802.

When American troops invaded Panama to oust Manuel Noriega, they found in the general's palace a tube of toothpaste from **Tom's of Maine.** Word does get around. This small, quirky firm, founded and still run by Tom Chappell, specializes in natural toothpastes made without artificial sweeteners (Chappell also makes natural mouthwashes, dental ribbon, shampoos, and deodorants). The toothpaste flavors tend toward the slightly offbeat and include "cinnamint," spearmint, and fennel. You'll find their taste tends to be more robust and less cloying than mainstream toothpastes. Commoners and dictators alike often find it hard to go back to their old brands once they've tried Tom's. The company is headquartered in the old train station in Kennebunk, just west of the tracks on Depot Street; look for a small sign. The outlet shop sells factory seconds (read: moderately crumpled toothpaste tubes) at a healthy discount. Open Monday through Saturday 9:00 A.M. to 4:30 P.M.

The **Seashore Trolley Museum,** located just north of Kennebunkport, may sound a bit dull to the uninitiated. It's easy to imagine a half dozen well-polished, lifeless streetcars housed in a trim building on a well-scrubbed, concrete floor. But do yourself a favor and check this out. It's anything but clean and trim. The museum seems a lively, thriving scrapyard where operating streetcars wind their way through heaps of rusting metal and piles of railroad ties. Wandering the grounds induces a sense of continual wonderment.

The museum, founded in 1939, contains the world's largest collection of streetcars, most of which have been restored and are now maintained by a cadre of two hundred volunteers, including many local retirees with a penchant for tinkering. The museum owns streetcars from New Orleans, Glasgow, Montreal, Rome, San Francisco, Budapest, and a number of towns in Maine. Each of the two hundred or so cars on the lot (of which forty run regularly) evokes a subtle nostalgia, even in those of us too young to remember the era when you could travel the entire eastern seaboard connecting one trolley line with the next. Some of the early cars still have the old advertising posters mounted inside. Most are housed in two corrugated metal sheds that produce a wonderfully cacophonous rattle when a breeze kicks up.

Admission includes unlimited rides along a 2-mile track through the woods. Be sure to visit the restoration shop, where new cars are overhauled when they arrive. (Average restoration time is four to seven years.) The gift shop offers an unrivaled selection of postcards, books, and other items related to streetcars.

The museum is 3.2 miles north of Kennebunkport on North Street. Open from late April through Columbus Day. During peak season (Memorial Day to Labor Day), the museum is open 10:00 A.M. to 5:30 P.M. (last ride is at 4:30 P.M.); limited hours during the shoulder seasons. Admission is $5.50 for adults, $3.50 for children aged six to sixteen, and free for children five and under and senior citizens sixty or older. Maximum charge per family is $18. For more information, call 967–2712.

Old Orchard Beach and Vicinity

Traveling anywhere in northern Maine or New Hampshire, you're likely to come across a sign pointing the way to Old Orchard Beach, located near the towns of Saco and Biddeford. This aggressive signing isn't the result of a hyperactive chamber of commerce. Thousands of French Canadians conduct annual pilgrimages to this lively summer town and its 7-mile beach, and you're as liable to hear French spoken as English. Old Orchard features an historic carousel and pier in addition to its hundreds of motels; but it is best known for its profusion of amusements, nausea-inducing rides, games of chance and skill, and foods cooked in oil. If you're an aficionado of the garish, plan to stroll after dark, when the beachfront fully displays its brilliant neon plumage.

Just over a mile to the south of Old Orchard on Route 9, you'll come to a suburb that has a decidedly different disposition. **Ocean Park** was founded in 1880 by the Centennial Conference of Free Will Baptists as an educational summer resort. In a stately grove of pines several blocks from the ocean, you'll find the three pleasing buildings from the colony's early days clustered on the north side of Temple Street near the intersection of Royal Street. Of particular interest is the Temple, an octagonal wooden structure representing an architectural style that was once highly popular. The building, based on plans purchased for $27, was dedicated in August 1881 and has been in continuous use by congregants since then.

Nearby, in Saco, is the York Institute, one of the region's best small museums. Well-designed displays highlight early life in southern Maine, with a particular emphasis on the late eighteenth and early nineteenth centuries. Founded in 1870, the museum features a colonial kitchen, an eighteenth-century bedroom, and an early printing press. An exceptional collection of paintings is also on display, including a fine selection of portraits. The museum is located at 371 Main Street in Saco, and admission is $1 for adults, 50 cents for children under twelve. Open May through October, Tuesday through Friday from 1:00 to 4:00 P.M. (until 8:00 P.M. on Thursdays); in July and August also open on Saturdays from 1:00 to 4:00 P.M. November through April the museum is open Tuesday and Wednesday from 1:00 to 4:00 P.M., Thursday from 1:00 to 8:00 P.M. For more information call 283–3861.

Inland York County

Far from the coast, in a wooded valley in the northwest part of the county, you'll find **Willowbrook at Newfield,** an historic village that offers visitors a glimpse of late nineteenth-century Maine. The museum opened in 1970 and consists of thirty-seven structures, including original homes and replicas of early buildings. The collections are extensive and broad, with virtually everything originating within 100 miles of the museum. Many of the items on display have been splendidly restored and refinished to their original luster, as if just from the shop of the craftsman.

The displays include sixty carriages and horse-drawn sleighs, an opulent 1849 Concord coach commissioned by a Bath sea captain, and an 1894 Armitage-Herschell carousel with the original organ. (The carousel operates, but rides aren't allowed.) A fine bicycle collection includes a curious tandem bicycle; it allows both front and back riders to steer, a mechanism that gives some pause. The centerpiece of the village is the 1835 William Duggin house, furnished in that cluttered Victorian style preferred by better families everywhere in the late nineteenth century. There's also a turn-of-the-century ice-cream parlor and a general store with penny candy that, remarkably, still costs a penny.

The emphasis at Willowbrook is on the late nineteenth century, but the one exhibit that may stick in your mind longest is Frank Skrobach's "roadable and garageable airplane," dating from the 1930s. Skrobach was an upstate New York inventor who keenly perceived that the main flaw of the airplane was its large wingspan: A pilot couldn't land on a highway since another plane might be coming the other way and they'd clip one another. Skrobach set about to remedy that. The result was an airplane with a 6-foot wingspan. Attached to a 21-foot zeppelin-shaped fuselage are not one but six pairs of wings. Diagrams show how the aerodynamics are supposed to work. In several early trials with a forty-five-horsepower engine, however, Skrobach's dream never got off the ground. Engineering students who've looked it over in recent years think the prototype would fly if equipped with a ninety-horsepower engine, but no flight tests are scheduled.

Willowbrook at Newfield is located just off Route 11 in New-field. (The turn is well marked.) The village is open between May 15 and September 30, 10:00 A.M. to 5:00 P.M. daily. Admission is $6 for adults, $3 for ages six to eighteen, and free for children under six. For more information call 793–2784.

CUMBERLAND COUNTY

Cumberland County is the most populous (around 250,000 residents), the wealthiest, and the most densely settled of Maine's counties. In some areas Cumberland flirts with a suburban tone, but generally it manages to retain its essential woodland character. In this the county is aided and abetted by miles of wooded shoreline along Casco Bay and by the dense forests in the hills around Sebago Lake, the state's second largest body of water.

Greater Portland

Portland, you'll read here and elsewhere, is the state's largest city. Don't be fooled by this "state's largest" business. It's still a small city, a pleasure to visit and a fine place to live. The city proper has a population of only 65,000 or so, making it about one-fifth as populous as Toledo, Ohio. If you count the surrounding communities, the metropolitan area climbs to only about 125,000, still small by national standards. Despite the relatively low head count, Portland has a brisk urban feel that eludes many other cities several times its size. That's due in large part to its location on a peninsula, which forced early builders to grow upwards rather than outwards. And Portland's urbanity transcends mere appearances. Today the city boasts its own symphony, a superb art museum, two theater groups, and an array of galleries and excellent restaurants.

Visitors invariably gravitate first to the Old Port near the waterfront, an area of brick sidewalks and cobblestone streets, chock full of boutiques, bars, tee-shirt shops, and ice-cream emporiums. These narrow streets blossomed during rediscovery and renewal in the late 1970s, when the run-down area was spruced up from sidewalk to cornice. Take some time to walk around the Old Port and investigate the extravagant late nineteenth-century brickwork on the buildings. If it seems somewhat uniform, it is; Portland's downtown was devastated by fire in 1866 and rebuilt shortly afterwards. Note that the dates on many of the buildings read 1867 or thereabouts.

The Old Port wears its charm on its sleeve, but the rest of the city's intrigue is somewhat more subtle. On upper Congress Street, Portland's main artery of commerce, visit the **Neal Dow Memorial,** a wonderful 1829 brick home preserved in memory of the man instrumental in bringing prohibition to Maine. Dow, who was born in Portland, grew up in a town that thrived on the rum trade with the West Indies. The obvious ill effects of "demon rum" on the city streets led Dow to become a lifelong temperance leader, and over time he became a surprisingly effective lobbyist. In 1851, Dow managed to usher through the state legislature a bill that effectively banned the sale of spirits in Maine. The campaign brought him political prominence and propelled him into the office of mayor of Portland. Not surprisingly, his actions also bred him a number of enemies. When touring the house, ask to see where local agitators tried to beat down the rear door to discuss some of their grievances with Mr. Dow.

When he died in 1897 (long after surviving a Civil War ordeal as a captured Union general at the age of fifty-eight), Dow bequeathed the mansion and its contents to the Maine Woman's Christian Temperance Union, which still maintains offices on the second floor. The union offers free tours of the first floor, which is kept up much as it was when Dow lived here. The shelves are lined with Dow's books on the evils of alcohol, and the several rooms are graced with a fine collection of priceless antiques. Another small room contains relics and artifacts from Dow's Civil War days.

The Dow Memorial, at 714 Congress Street, is open Monday through Friday 11:00 A.M. to 4:00 P.M. No admission is charged. Call 773–7773.

If the city's range of architecture intrigues you, consider a walking tour through one of several historic neighborhoods. Greater Portland Landmarks, a nonprofit group credited with curbing many of the excesses of urban renewal in recent decades, has produced a series of brochures highlighting four historic areas. One area is the Western Promenade, where the city's grandest homes stand on a bluff looking westward toward the White Mountains. The mansions range from Gothic to Italianate to shingle style, making the area a virtual catalog of nineteenth-century architectural styles. Around Bowdoin Street, note the grand shingle-style homes designed by renowned Portland architect John Calvin Stevens, including numbers 36, 40, 44, and 52.

Other walking tour brochures are available for the Old Port, State Street, and Congress Street. The cost is $1 each. Greater Portland Landmarks' headquarters is at 165 State Street and is open from 8:30 A.M. to 5:00 P.M. Monday through Friday. For more information call 774–5561.

Easily the most extravagant home in Portland is the **Morse-Libby House,** known locally as the Victoria Mansion. Built of brownstone in an exuberant interpretation of the Italianate villa style, the mansion was constructed between 1859 and 1863 for Ruggles Sylvester Morse, a Maine native who made his fortune in the New Orleans hotel trade. The exterior is solid and imposing, a layered grouping of towers and blocks with overhanging eaves. Inside, virtually no space has been left unadorned. Eleven Italian artists were employed to paint murals and trompe l'oeil scenes on the walls and ceilings; the staircases contain 400 hand-carved mahogany balusters. The dark, brooding rooms are filled with marble fireplaces and ornate chandeliers; stained glass brightens some of the darkness. Preservationists managed to forestall demolition of this gem (to make room for a gas station, no less) in 1940; the house is now administered by the Victoria Society of Maine.

Guided tours are offered between June and early October, Tuesdays through Saturdays 10:00 A.M. to 4:00 P.M. and Sundays 1:00 to 4:00 P.M. Admission is $4 for adults and $1.50 for children under eighteen. The mansion is at 109 Danforth Street between State and High streets. For more information call 772–4841.

A decidedly less opulent homestead is located not far away on busy Congress Street near Monument Square. The **Wadsworth-Longfellow House** was built in 1785–86 by General Peleg Wadsworth, a Revolutionary War officer and grandfather of Portland's most celebrated native son, Henry Wadsworth Longfellow. The poet spent his childhood in this house, which is as austere and simple as the Victoria Mansion is unrestrained. This was originally a two-story house, but its gabled roof was destroyed and a third story and hip roof added in 1815, creating a solid Federal appearance. Both the house and the gardens behind it are open to the public. The rooms are filled with furniture and documents related to the lives of the Wadsworths and the Longfellows. Immediately behind the home are the library and offices of the Maine Historical Society, where you can buy books on Maine history or indulge in local research (there's a small fee for nonmembers).

The Wadsworth-Longfellow House, at 485 Congress Street, is open June 1 through Columbus Day, Tuesday through Saturday 10:00 A.M. to 4:00 P.M. (Limited hours in October.) Admission is $3 for adults and $1 for children under twelve. For more information call 772–1807.

Continuing eastward on Congress Street you'll soon see the unique **Portland Observatory** on Munjoy Hill. This handsome conical building with a cupola atop was constructed in 1807 by Captain Lemuel Moody, and today it is the last signal tower remaining on the East Coast. Manned for many years by Moody himself, the wooden observatory was used to sight incoming cargo ships well before they pulled into the harbor. Once the ships were spotted, the observer would hoist the ship's flags atop the building to alert the town of its impending arrival. When it was built, the 86-foot-high observatory occupied an open, treeless hill used for political rallies, circuses, and public hangings. Today it is surrounded by an unassuming neighborhood of low apartment buildings and small shops.

Visitors climb to the top up a sturdy wooden staircase that passes through several levels, where windows offer glimpses of harbor and city. From the cupola and its open deck, visitors are rewarded with an extraordinary view northward up island-cluttered Casco Bay and westward to the White Mountains. The entire city seems to lie at your feet. With seagulls wheeling around and the views beyond Cushing Island to the open ocean beyond, it's a good reminder that Portland's history is inextricably bound with the sea.

The Observatory is at 138 Congress Street. When the flags are flying, it's open to visitors. Open weekends June through October, 1:00 to 5:00 P.M. From July through Labor Day, it's also open Wednesday through Sunday 1:00 to 5:00 P.M. Admission is $1.50 for adults, 50 cents for children under twelve. For more information call 774–5561.

The view from above may have stirred some curiosity about those islands on Portland's horizon. In fact, exploring the Casco Bay islands reveals a wholly different way of life. Although several

Portland Observatory, Portland

of the islands with year-round inhabitants—including Great and Little Diamond, Peaks, Long, and Cliff—are within Portland city limits, the pace is decidedly slower and the landscapes far more rural than urban.

Most of the islands entered their heyday as summer destinations for middle-class vacationers at the turn of the century, and the architecture reflects that heritage. There's typically a general store and maybe a small restaurant on each island, but little else. Most are still predominantly summer destinations with the exception of Peaks Island, which has become something of an island suburb; many of its inhabitants commute twenty minutes by ferry to jobs in the city. Chebeague Island, at 2,400 acres, is the largest and offers fine bicycling terrain. Cliff Island, where the movie *Whales of August* was filmed, is the farthest from town (over an hour by ferry) and has the most convincing lost-in-time atmosphere.

Frequent ferry service is offered throughout the summer to all islands; visitors can disembark with a picnic lunch to wander about and return on a later boat, or can simply enjoy the passing water view from benches on the top deck. The ferry terminal is located at the State Pier at the corner of Franklin and Commercial streets. For more information call Casco Bay Lines at 774–7871.

While on the waterfront, look for the **Lightship *Nantucket***, often docked near the State Pier. This handsome 150-foot boat, painted an unmistakable fire-engine red, was one of seventy lightships once stationed along the coast to warn mariners away from rocky shoals and other navigational hazards. The lightships—fitted with foghorns, bells, and powerful mast lights—were stationed where conditions prohibited construction of traditional lighthouses; the *Nantucket* spent much of her time near the treacherous Shoals of Nantucket off Massachusetts, manned by a crew who lived a life of boredom punctuated with moments of sheer terror. The *Nantucket* was tossed around in hurricanes in 1954 and 1959, the second of which dragged the ship and her two massive anchors some 80 miles off station. Things could have been worse; the ship's predecessor had been rammed and sunk on a foggy night in 1934 by the RMS *Olympia* (the *Titanic*'s sister ship), with seven crewmen perishing in the collision. By 1983 all U.S. lightships had been retired, replaced by large navigational buoys and Texas towers.

Forty-five-minute tours of the ship provide insight into the lonely, hazardous duty of a lightship crew. The cost is $3 for adults and $1.50 for children; the maximum for a family is $7. Open to the public in summer, Wednesday through Sunday 10:00 A.M. to 4:00 P.M.; in spring, weekends only. The *Nantucket* periodically sets off on tours of other New England ports or moves to other locations along the Portland waterfront. Call 775–1181 for current location.

Cape Elizabeth Area

Just across the harbor in South Portland you'll find the small but intriguing **Spring Point Museum,** located in the brick ordnance repair shop of former Fort Preble (1808–1950). This harborside museum opened in 1987 with exhibits on local sea culture and history, and through its rotating exhibits it provides some insight into the workings of the waterfront. In particular, you'll learn about the Liberty Ship era during World War II, when 236 of the ships were built in South Portland.

The museum's centerpiece is a curious bit of nautical archaeology: the copper-covered bow of the *Snow Squall,* an historic remnant from the last remaining American clipper ship. Built in South Portland in 1851, the ship was abandoned to rot on the Falkland Islands in 1864, but 35 feet of its 157-foot length were recovered and brought to the museum between 1982 and 1987. The conservation of the ship's bow is proceeding steadily if slowly; the process may be watched in a dim room kept moist and cool to arrest deterioration. This ship section is most of interest to nautical historians, but everyday visitors will be intrigued to see this work in progress. Afterwards, plan on a walk through the grounds of historic Fort Preble, then out on the breakwater to Spring Point Light.

The Spring Point Museum is open Memorial Day through October Wednesday through Sunday between 1:00 and 4:00 P.M. Admission is $2 for adults; children under twelve are free. The museum is at the end of Fort Road. Follow Broadway from South Portland to the marina, then turn right on Pickett Street. Fort Road is about a hundred yards on the left. For more information call 799–6337.

Not far from Spring Point is another new museum with a maritime theme. The **Museum at Portland Head Light** is located in the former keeper's quarters of a lighthouse commissioned by

George Washington. This venerable and handsome structure stands on a rocky promontory at the edge of a grassy park. It was completed in 1791 and occupied continuously until 1989; then the light was automated and the keeper's house decommissioned. The house and grounds have a rich history, including frequent visits by Henry Wadsworth Longfellow, who befriended the keepers and often walked here from Portland.

The museum, scheduled to open to the public in 1992, features displays and interpretive exhibits on the history of lighthouses and navigation through the ages. You'll learn about how mariners found their way along coasts from early Egypt to current times, when satellites have largely taken the place of the traditional visual guides. The museum's six rooms also include displays on regional history and commerce. The light tower itself, one of four nationwide that were commissioned by George Washington and have never been rebuilt, is still owned and operated by the Coast Guard and is not open to the public. Plan to bring a picnic when you visit; stunning views across open ocean and the islands of southern Casco Bay may be had from the grassy fields of surrounding Fort Williams Park, which has several picnic tables and charcoal grills. The park grounds are open daily from sunrise to 8:30 P.M.

The museum is operated by the town of Cape Elizabeth and is open in summer daily 10:00 A.M. to 4:00 P.M. Admission is $2. For more information call the town offices at 799–5251.

Northern Casco Bay

The town of Freeport is best known as the home of L. L. Bean, the famous retailer of outdoor gear and clothing. What started as a small shop specializing in leather-and-rubber boots for hunting has grown to the size of a regional shopping mall, with three levels of tents, hiking shoes, plaid shirts, khaki pants, winter jackets, and, of course, L. L. Bean hunting shoes. The store annually attracts thousands of shoppers, a fact that hasn't gone unnoticed by other retailers. In the last decade Freeport has assumed its place as a certified outlet mecca, offering everything from Dansk dinnerware to Patagonia outerwear. To its credit, the town has retained much of its original architecture and flavor, and shoppers can park once and visit most shops on foot. In recent months, however, outlet mania has started its southward creep along Route 1, and there's been a notable outbreak of massive parking lots. Although shopping opportunities are expanding, Freeport stands to lose the understated character and charm it's managed to preserve.

One spot in Freeport that hasn't been afflicted by progress is **Wolfe's Neck Farm,** easily one of the state's most scenic bits of agricultural land, located at the edge of the northwest Casco Bay. Visitors approach on a dirt road with broad views across pastures toward the water and to the islands and peninsulas beyond. This 600-acre alternative farm was founded in 1957 by Mr. and Mrs. L. M. C. Smith, both vigorous advocates of no-pesticide agricultural methods. The Smiths pioneered ecologically sound methods of raising beef, and in 1985 the farm was donated to the University of Southern Maine as a demonstration alternative farm. The university carries on the Smiths' doctrine, abstaining from pesticides and chemically refined fertilizers in raising summer and winter feed.

Visitors can stop by the gray clapboarded farmhouse to purchase their frozen USDA-inspected beef, which is offered in a variety of cuts. The beef contains less fat than most beef (which may translate into a slighter tougher cut) and has a beefier flavor than you're likely used to. The university also manages ninety campsites, including many along the tidal bay, for overnight tenting and motor home use. Camping fees are nominal. Also nearby is Wolfe's Neck Woods State Park, a 233-acre woodland park with a picnic area and several trails running through the forest and along the bay's edge. Open for day use from Memorial Day weekend through Labor Day.

To find the farm, head east on Bow Road from downtown Freeport for 2.4 miles, then make a right on Wolf Neck Road. After 1.7 miles, turn left on the dirt road and continue 0.6 miles to the farmhouse. The office is open for meat sales 8:00 A.M. to 4:30 P.M. Monday through Friday. Call 865–4469.

One of the more enduring and controversial historical figures in U.S. history is Admiral Robert E. Peary, putative discoverer of the North Pole and former resident of Casco Bay. Some hail him as one of America's greatest heroes; others dismiss him as an egomaniacal fraud. Recent photo analysis and exhaustive studies notwithstanding, no one seems to know for sure if Peary actually made it to the North Pole or doctored his calculations to make it appear that way. No matter where you stand on the debate, however, a couple of local attractions cast a light on the explorer's personality and achievements.

Located in the far reaches of Casco Bay, **Eagle Island** was Peary's summer home during and after his attempted conquests of the Pole. As a teenager growing up in Portland, he vowed one day to own the craggy seventeen-acre island. He accomplished this in 1879, purchasing it for $500. In 1904 he built a home here, which he expanded with a pair of imposing circular stone rooms in 1912.

Peary's heirs donated the island to the state, with much of the furniture from the years when the explorer occupied the place prior to his death in 1920. There are few formal exhibits, but enough furniture and household goods are present to convey a sense of Peary's character. Among the items on display are birds Peary collected as a young amateur taxidermist, as well as some of his later possessions. The upstairs bedrooms are creaky, small, and full of the smell of salt air. Be sure to leave time to wander the island; footpaths meander through forest and along rocky bluffs to the southern tip of the island, which has been taken over as a rookery by hundreds of gulls.

Eagle Island is open Memorial Day to Labor Day. Five moorings on the northwest side of the island are available to those traveling here on their own. Those without their own boats have two choices: From Freeport's town dock, Atlantic Seal Cruises offers two tours daily to the island with an hour's stopover. The fare is $15 for adults and $12 for children under twelve; call 865–6112. From Portland's waterfront, Eagle Tours leaves Long Wharf daily and includes a ninety-minute visit to the island. The fare is $15 for adults and $9 for children under nine. For more information call 774–6098.

If your curiosity about Peary and his exploits is piqued by Eagle Island, plan to visit the **Peary-MacMillan Arctic Museum,** located on the campus of Bowdoin College in Brunswick, a short drive north of Freeport. Housed on the first floor of distinguished Hubbard Hall, this thoroughly intriguing museum celebrates the Arctic accomplishments of Bowdoin alumni Peary and Donald MacMillan. In three exhibit rooms you'll get a good overview of their lives (MacMillan was on Peary's successful 1909 North Pole assault and subsequently became an able Arctic explorer in his own right) and view a number of the artifacts used during the attempts on the Pole, including dogsleds, snowshoes, and the gear used to make afternoon tea.

Other exhibits include a selection of items from the Arctic, ranging from stuffed birds such as the snowy owl, eider, and puffin to beautifully crafted Inuit snow goggles. Watch for the eerie tupilak carvings the Angmassalik Inuit created as effigies to bring harm to their enemies. On your way out note the Latin inscription carved in the lintel above the doorway: INVENIAM VIAM AUT FACIAM. According to Peary's biographer, the explorer penciled this motto above the bunk in his ship after losing most of his toes to frostbite during his unsuccessful 1899 expedition. From Seneca, it translates, "I shall find a way or make one."

The museum is open year-round Tuesday through Saturday 10:00 A.M. to 5:00 P.M. and on Sundays 2:00 to 5:00 P.M. Admission is free. For information call 725–3416.

Sebago Lake Region

Sebago Lake has long been a popular destination with summer folks who have ringed this massive lake with cabins and summer homes. A state park on the north end of the lake features a handsome white sand beach and provides access to swimmers and campers throughout the summer (693–6613). From Sebago Lake the Songo Locks connect to Brandy Pond and Long Lake at Naples, the former seat of amusement for the region. (Using a now-defunct canal from the coast, tourists could once travel by boat between Portland and Harrison at the north end of Long Lake.) Today the twenty-seven locks, first built in 1830, are in good working order and open and close constantly throughout the summer to accommodate the flow of canoes and motorboats and the Songo River Queen, an excursion boat based in Naples. The locks are located south of Naples en route to the state park.

In the rolling hills west of the lake, you may be surprised to come upon one of Maine's more striking museums. The **Jones Museum of Glass and Ceramics,** founded in 1978, is housed in a handsome dark green farm building dating from 1938 and set amid a hillside grouping of pleasing summer homes. Tall pines and open meadows surround the museum, which contains one of the more extraordinary collections of glass in the nation. You needn't be a glass connoisseur to enjoy an unhurried walk through this museum, just have an appreciation for form and color. The collections are as professionally curated and exhibited as at any major urban museum, with about six thousand objects on display (from a total collection of about seven thousand items) at any given time.

Rotating exhibits fill much of the first floor of the museum. These exhibits may feature historical displays, such as recent shows on Sandwich glass and marbles, or may highlight contemporary glassmakers and ceramicists, who seem constantly to push the boundaries with exuberant colors and fluid forms. The bulk of the museum's collections are exhibited on the second floor, where you may be surprised by the range and versatility of glass and ceramics. The collections vary in age from 1400 B.C. (Egyptian glass) to items not long out of the kiln or glassblower's shop. You'll also gain insight into the social and economic contexts of glassmaking through exhibits that include everything from a glass mailbox to intricately detailed teapots to attractive embalming-fluid bottles. Another exhibit area challenges viewers to spot the differences between reproductions and originals.

The Jones Museum also has a 5,000-book library that is open to the public for research, as well as an extensive gift shop offering antique originals (no reproductions) and reference works. Lectures on glassmaking and ceramics are scheduled throughout the year.

Open May through mid-November Monday through Saturday 9:30 A.M. to 5:00 P.M. and on Sundays from 1:00 to 5:00 P.M. Admission is $2.50 for adults, $1.50 for students, and 50 cents for children under twelve. The museum is located off Route 107 just south of the town of Sebago. Look for roadside markers. For more information call 787–3370.

Just up the hill from the Jones Museum is Douglas Mountain, a hilltop Nature Conservancy preserve that makes a fine destination for a picnic on a clear day. This 169-acre parcel features a pair of undemanding trails running 0.25 mile to the 1,415-foot summit. On the top of the rocky hill is a 16-foot stone tower, built in 1925 by the land's former owner, a surgeon who found relaxation in stonework. The top of the tower offers commanding views of the entire region, across Lake Sebago and Casco Bay to the east and westward to the Presidential Range of the White Mountains in New Hampshire. Nearby a sizable boulder has been carved with the phrase, NON SIBI SED OMNIBUS ("not for one but for all"). Visitors in late summer will be rewarded with an ample crop of wild blueberries and blackberries along the trails near the ridge.

New Gloucester Region

Eight miles north of Gray on Route 26 you'll pass a handsome assortment of brick and clapboard buildings on a gentle rise amid open meadows and orchards. That's the **Sabbathday Lake Shaker Community,** the last active Shaker community in the nation. As of 1991 some nine Shakers lived in these venerable buildings on 1,900 acres originally settled in 1793 by Shakers carrying on the traditions of Mother Ann Lee and her disciples. These traditions include an emphasis on simplicity in their lives and crafts, a commitment to industry ("hearts to God and hands to work"), and celibacy. The latter, which seems to attract the most attention from visitors, raises the question of how the community has managed to propagate itself for nearly two hundred years. The answer: For many years the Shakers adopted orphans. Several of the older sisters present today were themselves adopted. After this practice was disallowed by the state, the community became dependent on converts to carry on their work. Today several of the more committed Shakers are in their thirties.

The Shakers—who are all too frequently confused with Quakers—received their name from the dances they once executed during their religious celebrations. The practice was discontinued around 1900 in deference to the older Shaker members. In addition to their religious ceremonies, the Shakers are best known for their furniture and baskets, which display an unmatched devotion to practicality and simplicity.

A good introduction to the Shaker life and tradition may be had through one of the tours of the village offered daily except Sunday throughout the summer. Nine of the buildings were constructed before 1850, and all are possessed of an unvarnished grace and refinement. Of particular note is the meetinghouse, built in 1794 and still used for Sunday services in summer (the public is invited). The downstairs room is spare and open; the light streaming in through the windows seems part of the design. Examples of fine woodworking are displayed throughout several buildings, representing a variety of Shaker communities. You can identify each chair's provenance by the finials, which were unique for each community. The museum also displays examples of later Shaker craftsmanship and design, some of which display a mild but startling flirtation with Victorian ornamentation. Be

**Waiting room at Shaker Community,
Sabbathday Lake**

sure to stop at the gift shop, where you can buy herbs grown in
the community's garden and sold here since 1799.

An introductory tour of the village (about one hour) costs $3;
an extended tour (one hour and forty-five minutes) costs $4.50.
Open Memorial Day to Columbus Day (closed Sundays) 10:00 A.M.
to 4:30 P.M. For more information call 926–4597.

Off the Beaten Path in the Western Mountains

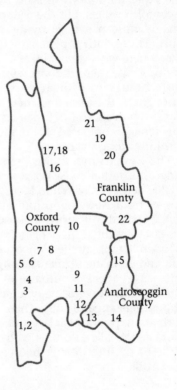

1. Admiral Peary House
2. Clarence Mulford Room
3. Quisisana
4. Westways
5. Evans Notch
6. Telemark Inn
7. Moses Mason House
8. Bryant Pond Telephone Museum
9. Perham's of West Paris
10. Strathglass Park Historic District
11. Paris Hill
12. State of Maine Building
13. Moxie Capital of the World
14. Bates College
15. Norlands Living History Center
16. Stephen Phillips Memorial Preserve
17. Saddleback Mountain
18. Orgonon
19. Sugarloaf U.S.A.
20. Stanley Museum
21. Widow's Walk
22. Nordica Homestead

WESTERN MOUNTAINS

In their haste to visit the White Mountains of New Hampshire and the Green Mountains of Vermont, many visitors to New England overlook the mountains of western Maine. These rolling, rugged hills haven't developed quite the popular mythology of the other mountains, nor do they offer as broad a range of services for travelers. But the region is well worth visiting for its dramatic landscapes, quiet byways, and vast lakes set amid forested hills. Those with a penchant for outdoor activities will feel at home here with canoe, bike, or hiking shoes. Those whose inclinations take them indoors will also find plenty to do, from historic homes to offbeat museums. Fine inns may be found throughout the area, and there's excellent browsing at unassuming antiques shops (Victorian antiques seem to be the standard in this region, compared to the more common Federal and Empire furniture along the coast).

The western mountains aren't defined by a single mountain range, but rather consist of a series of hills and watersheds. Some 50,000 acres of the White Mountain National Forest slip over the border from New Hampshire into Maine, then unravel into the gentle Oxford Hills. The Mahoosuc Range passes near Bethel and is traversed by the Appalachian Trail; those who've hiked the entire 2,100-mile trail say the Mahoosucs contain some of the most difficult and dramatic segments along the entire route. From the summit of Old Speck Mountain on a clear day you can see Mount Blue, an almost perfectly pyramidal hill 32 miles away in the heart of another range of hills. There's also the Rangeley Lake region, with its network of lakes and mountains, and the impressive Carrabasset Valley, dominated by the Bigelow Range, which offers some of the best Maine hiking opportunities outside of Baxter State Park.

OXFORD COUNTY

Oxford County extends narrowly along Maine's western edge from the village of Porter to the Canadian border, far into timberland territory. The county tends to be rough-hewn in its geography and culture, with extraordinary gems—both literal and figurative—dispersed throughout.

White Mountains Region

Fryeburg is a modest town of broad streets and open views located on the heavily traveled route between Portland and North Conway, New Hampshire. Best known for the Fryeburg Fair—Maine's largest county fair, held annually at the end of September—Fryeburg also lies on the Saco River, Maine's most popular (and populous) canoeing route. Several canoe liveries may be found in and around Fryeburg, offering canoe rentals and shuttles up and down the river. The Saco is distinguished by almost constant sandbars, which invite leisurely excursions with frequent stops. Be forewarned that the river is exceedingly popular on weekends, and some sandbars may offer all the remote wilderness character of New York's Jones Beach. If you don't feel like hassling with a canoe, there's easy access to one large sandbar on Route 113 north of town. Park in the lot just north of the bridge and walk down to the river.

On Elm Street in Fryeburg, you'll find the **Admiral Peary House,** a pleasant bed and breakfast inn. As a recent college graduate, Arctic explorer Robert Peary lived quietly here in 1877–79 while employed as a land surveyor. He had pleasant memories of Fryeburg, where he spent his idle time practicing taxidermy. The exterior of the house retains its nineteenth-century farmhouse charm, but Peary certainly wouldn't recognize the interior if he were to visit today. Owners Nancy and Ed Greenberg have built four modern and comfortable guest rooms with private baths in the attached barn, and have added other amenities such as a clay tennis court, a hot tub, and a spacious country kitchen, where breakfasts are served in inclement weather. A comfortable deck overlooks the well-landscaped yard, and the guests' living room features a fireplace and an antique billiards table. The best room in the house is the "North Pole," located in the former attic, with Palladian windows offering a view out toward Stark Mountain. The guest rooms have more privacy than at many B&Bs, and guests are provided with a filling breakfast in the morning.

Rates run between $87 and $96, depending on the room. The inn (reservations required; no smokers, please) is at 9 Elm Street. For more information call 935–3365.

Peary wasn't the only person of note to call Fryeburg home. In this century author Clarence E. Mulford (1883–1956) lived here—not on a rugged butte in Utah—while writing his Hopalong Cassidy novels. A collection of his works and a sampling of memorabilia is housed in the **Clarence Mulford Room** at the Fryeburg Public Library. This reading room has a portrait of Mulford as well as displays of historic western guns (including a buffalo gun), model ships and stage coaches, and a case of Mulford's collected works, including editions in Czech, Danish, and Finnish. The library, in the former schoolhouse at 98 Main Street, is sturdily constructed of granite blocks and stays cool even during the dog days of summer.

Heading northward from Fryeburg, you have a choice of two routes, both appealing. You can either drive north along Route 5 on the east side of Kezar Lake, or follow ever-narrowing Route 113 through scenic Evans Notch. The first route gives access to two venerable lakeside resorts; the second offers a network of excellent hiking trails to the summits of open mountains.

Kezar Lake, bounded to the west by unspoiled mountains, is regarded by many as the state's most perfect lake. It's also one of its least accessible. (This, in fact, may be *why* it's considered a nearly perfect lake.) Public roads touch upon the lake only at a crossing called "the Narrows," so the best views are reserved for those owning summer homes hereabouts—author Stephen King among them. Fortunately, there are a couple of options for those without the good sense to be born into a family with a Lake Kezar summer home.

For those with musical inclinations, there's **Quisisana,** a rustic lakeside resort set amid towering white pines. Here you're as liable to hear an aria emanating from the forest as the muffled call of a mourning dove. Since 1945 Quisisana has offered its guests both superb cuisine and a varied musical menu, with selections ranging from opera to popular show tunes. Owner Jane Oran recruits her summer staff from conservatories around the nation, and the students make beds, wait on tables, and perform nightly in the vintage wooden recital hall with dramatic views down the lake. Up to 150 guests reside in cozy white cabins scattered about the grounds and along the lakeshore, occupying their days with swimming, sunning, canoeing, and exploring the surrounding hills. Extra recitals are sometimes also scheduled for rainy-day diversions.

The musical repertory schedule is designed around a week-long stay, but shorter visits can sometimes be accommodated early in the season. Quisisana is 3.5 miles north of Lovell; look for road-side signs as you approach. Rates range from $85 to $125 per person per day including all meals and entertainment. For more information call 925–3500.

The only sounds at **Westways,** just a few miles up the lake, is provided by the loons on the lake and wind rattling through the poplars. Built in the 1920s ostensibly as a corporate retreat for the Diamond Match Company, the lodge was used primarily as the private getaway for the family of the company president, William Fairburn. The man had taste, if not exacting scruples. The lodge is filled with dark wood and creaky floors, richly colored carpets and regal furniture. With only seven rooms, guests are well pampered here. Cocktails are served each evening at the boathouse, and breakfasts are enjoyed on the enclosed porch. Reserve the "master bedroom" for extraordinary views down the lake, along with carved wooden bookcases, an oak bed, and a wonderful 1920s-style bathroom with some quirky features, including a writing desk above the bath tub. (One theory is that Fairburn liked to soak his feet while he wrote.) A small beach with canoes is a short walk down a pathway through a patch of blueberry bushes. There's also a vintage recreation hall with a two-lane bowling alley and billiards, and a shingled indoor "fives" court used for handball.

The well-regarded dining room seats forty, and dinners are served to the public by reservation. Such opulence doesn't come cheap. For the master bedroom rates are $195 per night for two, including breakfast and dinner. (A smaller room may be had for $105 with breakfast only.) Several modern vacation homes located on the former estate grounds are available for rent by the week. For more information call 928–2663.

If you opt to head north on Route 113, you'll first drive through farmlands with open vistas of distant ridges. But soon enough those ridges start to converge at **Evans Notch,** and the valley becomes pinched and narrow, as does the road itself when you enter the national forest. As you climb, views of the valley open up, with glimpses of the scraggy peaks above you. The forest is dense with birch, beech, and maple trees, which often overarch the road to create a shady canopy.

If you're so inclined, set out on one of the hiking trails to these ridges for sweeping views of western Maine and the taller peaks of the Carter and Presidential ranges. A list of suggested hikes is available from the U.S. Forest Service's office in Bethel. (Write to: Evans Notch Ranger Station, RFD 2, Box 2270, Bethel, ME 04217.) One hike that may be accomplished in a couple of hours without map or guide is to the summit of East Royce Mountain. This 1.3-mile trail ascends steadily through hardwoods and along an attractive brook, ending at open granite ledges with excellent views across rolling hills toward Kezar Lake. The trailhead, with parking for about twenty cars, is on the west side of Route 113 just north of where the road begins its descent toward the town of Gilead. The trail is well marked.

If you'd rather not serve as your own beast of burden, consider signing up for llama trekking at the **Telemark Inn.** This distinguished inn, housed in a summer retreat built by a wealthy businessman in 1900, is located deep in the countryside near Bethel on the eastern edge of the White Mountains. Steve Crone, the owner, was the first White Mountain entrepreneur to offer this pleasurable way of visiting the mountains. Llamas, unintimidating ruminants, have a calming affect on hypertense executives and hyperactive children alike. Crone offers day trips as well as overnight excursions, with varied destinations that include open mountaintops and riverside glens. Catered gourmet lunches are an option for those pressed for time. Those wishing to take a bit more time to get to know the area and the habits of these gentle Andean creatures might consider the five-day package, which includes a lake excursion by canoe as well as a llama-attended overnight in the mountains. Children may lead their own llamas if they so desire; otherwise handlers take care of the animals.

Rates for the trips range from $70 for a catered day trip to $750 per adult ($550 per child under fourteen) for the week-long mountain-and-lake trip. For more information contact Steve at 836–2703.

If you're equipped for camping, there are several U.S. Forest Service campgrounds in the Evans Notch region, but none as quiet and remote as the Crocker Pond campground located down a dirt road south of Bethel. With only eight campsites, it often fills on weekends but remains out-of-the-way enough that sites are generally available during the week. Several quiet ponds in the area are suitable for fishing, and a couple of hiking trails near the campsite provide access to the backcountry. For more information on this campground or recreational opportunities, contact the Forest Service's Evans Notch Ranger Station in Bethel at 824–2134.

Bethel Area

Heading northeast of the Evans Notch region, you'll soon arrive at the dignified town of Bethel, full of white clapboard and abounding with evidence of a comfortable, prosperous history. A number of attractive early homes front the Bethel Common—an elongated greensward with benches and a fountain—as does the venerable Bethel Inn, long a destination for those seeking respite from sultry eastern cities. The inn was built by the famous neurologist Dr. John Gehring, who also opened the nearby Gehring Clinic, a treatment center for nervous disorders. (Bethel once was referred to as "the resting place of Harvard" because of the high proportion of patients from Cambridge's academic community.) Nearby are the tasteful brick buildings of Gould Academy, a respected private secondary school founded in 1836.

Facing the common you'll also see the simple but distinguished **Moses Mason House,** now owned and operated by the Bethel Historical Society. This 1813 Federal-style house with the characteristic fan over the front door was built by Dr. Moses Mason (1789–1866), one of Bethel's early civic leaders. The house is believed to be the first in the district to be painted white, and the first built on a stone foundation; locals told Mason the wind would certainly blow it over. Mason served not only as town doctor but as postmaster and justice of the peace. The original contents of the house were auctioned off in the 1970s, but many of these items are finding their way back through local donation. The house and its intricate woodwork are meticulously maintained, with period furniture filling the rooms.

If you're in the least interested in American primitive painting or the history of decorative arts, the front hallway alone is worth the price of admission. The walls of the entryway and the second-floor landing are covered with a sweeping paint-on-plaster mural attributed to well-known primitive painter, Rufus Porter. A seascape with boat at anchor graces the first floor; along the stairs and on the second floor is a forest scene, dense with the delicately wrought boughs of white pines. The walls were first painted a century and a half ago, and they have never been papered or painted over, yielding one of the best examples of early decorative painting in the state. Be sure to note also the intriguing chair built by Mason, made of curly maple, crushed velvet, and moosehorn.

The Moses Mason House is open in July and August daily except Mondays, 1:00 to 4:00 P.M. Admission is $1.50 for adults and 75 cents for children. For more information call 824–2908.

Oxford Hills

The town of Bryant Pond will forever occupy a curious footnote in the annals of modern American communications, for it was the last town in the United States to rely on the old crank phones. These rather primitive phones, called "magnetos," connected the denizens of the village with the outside world until October 1983. Up until then, any Bryant Ponder wishing to place a call cranked their phone to contact the operator, who then patched it through. The local telephone company was located in its owner's living room, where operators inserted the proper jack in the proper hole. Picturesque but cumbersome, the massive and archaic switchboard was finally replaced with more modern switching apparatus during a nationally publicized transition.

Not wanting to let this bit of history slip by, local residents created a sort of shrine to the switchboard: The **Bryant Pond Telephone Museum.** In addition to housing the nation's last operating switchboard, the museum can make a couple of other notable claims: It may very well be the smallest museum in the nation (measuring not much more than 12 by 15 feet), and it certainly has among the most limited hours (open only on the last Saturday in September). Inside you'll find the old switchboard, along with some early phones, the operators' chairs, and a small assortment of crank phone memorabilia. Next door is a windowless concrete telephone switching building painted the neutral color of a Band-Aid, representing today's faceless but infinitely more efficient state of communications arts.

If you can't wait until September, the museum is also open by appointment. Call 336–9911. The museum is located on Rumford Road 0.8 mile north of Route 26.

Oxford County has long been renowned for its deposits of rare minerals, including fine grades of tourmaline prized by gemologists. To learn more about local minerals, plan a stop at **Perham's of West Paris,** one of the nation's preeminent destinations for rockhounds. Founded by Stanley Perham in 1919, this rock shop has just about everything for the inveterate collector of minerals and gemstones. A wide array of rare crystals and other minerals from around the world are for sale, displayed neatly in glass shelves and white cardboard boxes. For neophytes a small museum provides a fine overview of what's what in Maine, including several remarkable samples of elusive watermelon tourmaline, a delicate crystal of smoky pink ringed with a thin rind of emerald green. For those who prefer the finished product, Perham's also has an extensive jewelry selection.

Perham's owns five quarries within 10 miles of the shop, which are open to rock collectors (four are free; a $1 charge is levied at the fifth). The quarries invariably yield something intriguing and are a popular destination with families looking for an inexpensive and enjoyable way to while away a sunny afternoon. Ask for a quarry map at Perham's front counter.

Perham's is endlessly patient with novices, but it caters to the experienced collector as well, selling prospecting hammers and chisels, detailed field guides, lapidary equipment, metal detectors, and gold panning dishes. Even if you're not a committed rockhound, browsing is entertaining and provides a glimpse into the intriguing subculture of the rock collector. A poem posted on the back wall may sum up the outsider's view:

> *I think that there shall never be*
> *An ignoramus just like me*
> *Who roams the hills throughout the day,*
> *To pick up rocks that do not pay.*
> *For there's one thing I've been told*
> *I take the rocks and leave the gold.*

Perham's is open 9:00 A.M. to 5:00 P.M. daily, except on Thanksgiving and Christmas. The shop is located on the north side of Route 26 near the village of West Paris. For more information call 674–2341.

If rock collecting remains baffling but the search for gold makes perfect sense, try your hand at gold panning in the Swift River around Roxbury and Byron. The nation's first gold strike was said to have been in Byron, and since then the river has regularly if hesitantly given up small amounts of glistening gold flakes and an infrequent nugget. In the last century the area hosted periodic gold booms, particularly after the 1849 San Francisco Gold Rush put everyone in the mind of making a quick fortune in mining. Under such mass delusion, a number of "paper mines" and fraudulent corporations were created, enriching the unscrupulous and impoverishing the gullible and the greedy alike.

You can pick up a gold panning dish and any of several books on panning technique at Perham's. If you'd like a more personal introduction, contact Greg Willet (864–3717), who's based in Rangeley. A young professional prospector, Willet has experience in working claims in Maine and around the country. As his collection of local nuggets and gold flakes attests, he knows where to go and what to look for. Willet offers half-day panning lessons as well as full-day expeditions using sluice boxes and portable dredges. He provides the basic panning equipment (which you keep at the end of the day) and this unique guarantee: You'll find gold, or he'll give you some of his own. Even if your expedition doesn't pay for itself with a major strike, a day prospecting is one of the best ways to enjoy an afternoon along a remote stretch of river. Half-day expeditions range from $65 to $75, depending on which river you visit, and full-day trips from $130 to $150.

In the industrial town of Rumford, where the downtown is located on an island in the shadow of a Boise Cascade paper mill, you'll find the vestiges of an enlightened experiment in corporate paternalism dating from the turn of the century. The **Strathglass Park Historic District** consists of fifty-one elegant brick buildings located in a parklike setting amid pines and silver maples on a hillside across from the mill. The neighborhood's character is sort of Birmingham, England, by way of Boston's Beacon Hill.

The homes were built in 1901–02 by Hugh Chisholm, a principal in the Oxford Paper Company (later to be taken over by Boise Cascade). Appalled by the living conditions of many company workers, and hoping to attract a more qualified work force, Chisholm commissioned a New York architect to design these spacious duplexes surrounded by broad lawns. Workers nominated by their foremen were given first crack at renting the new homes at reasonable rates, for which all services were provided. The company sold off the buildings in the late 1940s, and today they are all privately owned. For the most part they remain in good condition. To reach Strathglass Park, turn off Route 2 uphill on Main Street, then make the next right between the tall stone columns.

Another intriguing historic setting, albeit from an earlier age, may be found in southern Oxford County, not far from Route 26. **Paris Hill** is notable both for its assortment of handsome Federal-style homes and as the birthplace of Hannibal Hamlin, a Maine political icon and vice president under Abraham Lincoln during his first term. This ridgetop setting, with views toward the White Mountains, serves as a fine backdrop for an uncommonly well-preserved village of nineteenth-century houses. With the highway some distance away, it also has a dignified country feel that in other towns has been compromised by the noisy persistence of the automobile and the relentless widening of roads.

The Hamlin Memorial in Paris Hill is located adjacent to Hannibal Hamlin's grand estate on the village green and is the only building open to the public. This stout granite building served as a local jail between 1822 and 1896. In 1901 it was purchased by one of Hamlin's descendants and converted into a library and museum, which it remains to this day. The museum displays examples of early American primitive art, local minerals, and items related to Hamlin's life. Open Tuesday through Friday 10:00 A.M. to 4:00 P.M.; Saturday 10:00 A.M. to 2:00 P.M.; and Wednesday evening 7:00 to 9:00 P.M.

ANDROSCOGGIN COUNTY

Androscoggin County tends to fall between the cracks. It's not in the Casco Bay region, but neither is it in the Oxford Hills or the Kennebec Valley. I've included it in the Western Mountains section because many people travel through the county en route to the mountains from the coast. Don't rush the trip; this small county can best be appreciated at a slow pace.

Poland Spring Area

Just north of the Sabbathday Lake Shaker Community (see page 28) in Cumberland County, you'll cross the county line and come to Poland Spring. Actually, there's a good chance you'll drive through it without noticing it. History is strong here, but a town center is not.

41

Poland Spring gained worldwide fame in the nineteenth century for its waters. In 1794 Jabez Ricker of Alfred, Maine, purchased this land with its fine spring from the Shakers and established his farm and an inn for travelers. Business was steady if not spectacular for half a century, until Jabez's son, Hiram, became convinced that the waters from the spring had cured him of chronic dyspepsia. The spring soon became well known for its healing abilities, and by 1876 the Rickers advertised their water as "a sure cure for Bright's Disease of the kidneys, stone in the bladder and kidneys, liver complaint, dropsy, salt, rheum, scrofula, humors, and all diseases of the urinary organs." A sprawling grand hotel with sweeping views of the Oxford Hills was built in 1875, with the famous waters pumped into the hotel via a steam pump. At its pinnacle the resort boasted a 200-foot dining room and a fireplace that consumed 6-foot logs. The complex also included a number of spacious annexes and outbuildings for guests and staff.

Much of the resort's history may be seen in exhibits in the **State of Maine Building,** located on the grounds of the former Poland Spring Hotel. This turreted stone building was constructed for the 1893 Chicago World's Fair, where it was used to display Maine's products. After the exposition the Rickers dismantled the building, shipped it to Maine, and rebuilt it on their grounds as the resort library.

Today the building contains fascinating memorabilia of the Poland Spring Hotel, including a model of the main hotel (which burned to the ground in 1975), early photographs, and examples of dinnerware and other accouterments of resort life. Detailed cardboard models of architecturally significant buildings of Maine, constructed by Larry Smith, are on the third floor. The building itself is an architectural gem, with an open, courtyardlike interior and a lacy weblike skylight brightening the dark woodwork.

Incidentally, Poland Spring water is still available nationwide, although the claims for its powers have been tempered somewhat. (It cures thirst, but little else.) Perrier, the French mineral water company, now owns the facility and pumps the water in a modern and hygienic nearby plant that is not open to the public.

The State of Maine Building is open in July and August Friday through Monday 9:30 A.M. to 3:30 P.M., and Tuesday, Wednesday, and Thursday 9:30 A.M. to noon. Open June and September on

Maine State Building, Poland Spring

weekends only, 9:30 A.M. to 3:30 P.M. Admission is $1; children under fifteen free. Located on Route 26; look for signs.

Lewiston-Auburn and Vicinity

Not far from Poland Spring is the unassuming town of Lisbon Falls, dominated by formidable brick factory buildings along the Androscoggin River. In a small storefront in the center of town, you'll find a somewhat peculiar shrine to another beverage that claimed to be a curative elixir.

In 1885 Dr. Augustin Thompson—a native of Union, Maine—patented and began producing something called Moxie Nerve Food. Thompson, a master of marketing, claimed that the secret to the beverage had been obtained by one Lieutenant Moxie. Adventurer Moxie had witnessed South American Indians consuming the juice of a certain plant, which infused them with preternatural strength. The miraculous plant was brought back, or so the story went, and given to Dr. Thompson, who distilled this beverage and named it after its discoverer. Thompson claimed that Moxie would "cure brain and nervous exhaustion, paralysis, loss of manhood, softening of the brain and mental imbecility." So popular was Moxie that its name soon entered the English language, becoming synonymous with pluck and courage. Moxie was the soft drink of choice throughout New England in the first part of this century until it was eclipsed by Coca-Cola, which now owns the name and manufactures the product.

Where does Lisbon Falls come into this tale? Through the door of Frank Anicetti's Kennebec Fruit Store, otherwise known as the **Moxie Capital of the World.** Anicetti's store, opened by his grandfather in 1914, has become a virtual Moxie museum, housing a wide selection of Moxie paraphernalia (cassettes, T-shirts, and books) and other items of interest to Moxie aficionados. In addition, Anicetti sells his own Moxie ice cream, which he says is not available anywhere else, and is willing to talk about Moxie and its history longer than perhaps any other living human being. The store is also headquarters for the Moxie Festival, held annually in mid-July. (For the exact date, check with the Lisbon Area Chamber of Commerce at 353–5026.) Anicetti's store is located at the corner of Route 196 and Main Street in downtown Lisbon Falls.

The twin cities of Lewiston-Auburn form the commercial center of Androscoggin County, making up Maine's second largest urban area after Portland. The area was widely known in the last century and beyond as one of the shoe-making capitals of New England; during World War I 75 percent of all canvas shoes in the world were made in Lewiston. Vestiges of Lewiston's boom times are clearly seen in the vast, Dickensian factory buildings lining the river's edge. Between the two cities the Androscoggin tumbles over a series of falls, and during spring runoff it presents a gloriously tumultuous display. West Pitch Park on the Auburn side of the river is a fine place to view both the cataracts and Lewiston's historic skyline of square factories punctuated with soaring spires.

Indeed, you might find it worthwhile to visit the spires at the Church of Saints Peter and Paul, an imposing Gothic edifice that looms over the city and lends it a distinctly European flavor. The church, built during the Great Depression, is a proud testament to Lewiston's fiercely Catholic French-Canadian population, which settled here in great number during the cities' glory days. This church is notable for a pair of 168-foot towers made of Maine granite and a magnificent, lofty nave with a lovely rose window. After years of deterioration an extensive $2 million restoration was launched in the late 1980s.

Also in Lewiston is the campus of **Bates College,** a distinguished four-year liberal arts school that can claim Edmund Muskie and Bryant Gumbel among its alumni. Bates began more than a century ago as a Baptist seminary; it subsequently expanded both its academic mission and its campus. Many distinctive buildings grace the attractive grounds, which are overarched with an abundance of trees. Worth visiting is the modern Olin Arts Center, where community performances are staged and the college's permanent collection is often on display. Paintings include several by Marsden Hartley, a Lewiston native who went on to international acclaim for his bold, colorful landscapes.

Livermore Area

Maine's numerous historic homes and buildings—from Kittery to Madawaska—provide many a good vantage point to view the state's past. But one destination near the town of Livermore offers more than just a view. It offers a chance to travel back in time; more precisely, a chance to experience life on a Maine farm circa 1870.

Norlands Living History Center with its weekend programs called "adult live-ins" occupies a special niche in the "adventure travel" market. Between four and fifteen guests arrive on Friday afternoon at the elaborate, Italianate farmhouse surrounded by 445 acres of forest and farmland—and live another life through Monday afternoon. Guests assume the identity of an historic character associated with the farm; they even have the option of donning vintage farm clothes. Guests don't exactly experience the rose-tinted bucolic life celebrated by nineteenth-century poets, however. There's little time for reading sonnets beneath an applewood bower. Living in the last century means sleeping on a corn-husk and straw mattress atop a rope bed in a room with peeling paint and plaster, pumping water into a basin for your morning ablutions, and assisting with the slaughter to put food on the table. Don't look for a restful vacation so much as for a remarkably in-depth education. (There are *some* concessions to modernity: Modern toilet paper augments the corn husks supplied in the outhouses.)

During the course of the long weekend, guests (both men and women) labor in the fields, tend the horse and oxen, do the cooking on a massive Queen Atlantic wood stove, and work on quilts. They also visit a school, using quills and inkpots in the lessons, and research the history of their characters in early farm documents.

Whether you make an extended visit as a "live-in" or just drop by for a two-hour tour, you'll certainly come to feel you know the Washburn family, who built this farm in the wilds of Maine early in the last century. In the Gothic library you'll hear stories about the fantastically successful Washburn sons; they built the library as a memorial to their parents. Three of the brothers served in the U.S. Congress simultaneously (representing three different states), a feat that has not been duplicated by any family since.

In July and August Norlands offers frequent tours, which include a lesson at the schoolhouse. Tours are held everyday between 10:00 A.M. and 4:00 P.M. and cost $4.50 for adults and $2.50 for children. Norlands is located on Norlands Road (off Route 108), northeast of Livermore and south of Livermore Falls. For more information on the live-in program (a three-night stay

with all meals costs about $200) or special events, call 897–4366
or write the center at RR 2, Box 1740, Livermore Falls, ME 04254

FRANKLIN COUNTY

Rugged Franklin County includes Mount Blue, Rangeley Lake, the
Carrabassett Valley, and a host of remote villages, each with
nothing more than a general store and a video shop. Accommodations range from high luxury to basic necessities, but the landscapes and bountiful wildlife are uniformly enchanting.

Rangeley Lakes Region

Driving northward on Route 17 from the towns of Rumford and
Mexico, you'll soon come to a point known locally as "Height of
Land." You'll know when you've arrived. After following the
twisting road as it ascends the rolling hills, you'll soon find
Mooselookmeguntic Lake suddenly at your feet, massive,
indomitable, and (most likely) stippled with whitecaps. The view
is perhaps the most spectacular in Maine, made all the more so
because it comes so unexpectedly.

The far lakeshore and two of the largest islands clearly visible
at the southern end of the lake—Toothaker and Students—are
part of a private wilderness preserve. Private, but open to the
public. The **Stephen Phillips Memorial Preserve** was
founded two decades ago by Phillips (since deceased), who feared
the twin threats of commercial development and state management. His concerns about development proved well founded:
Much of Mooselookmeguntic's shoreline was subdivided and
developed for second homes during the real estate frenzy of the
1980s. The dozens of miles of lakeshore and island property in
the preserve are maintained in a natural state and offer some of
the more scenic and wild landscapes in the state. A handful of
the lakeside campsites are within short walking distance from a
car, but the majority of the sixty maintained campsites are accessible only by boat. Canoes may be rented at the the preserve
headquarters, which has a canoe launching ramp.

Camping fees are $6 per night for two people; children are $2
additional. Reservations are accepted by mail or by phone

(864–2003). If you don't have reservations, a wooden board near the preserve headquarters is adorned with color-coded washers indicating available, occupied, and reserved sites.

If you'd rather travel by foot than canoe, a number of excellent hikes are available in the Rangeley region. For starters, you might hike the mile-long trail to the open summit of Bald Mountain, located on Mooselookmeguntic's lakeshore near Oquossoc; look for trail signs on the lakeshore road 1 mile south of Haines Landing. For the more ambitious, a hike along the Appalachian Trail to the top of **Saddleback Mountain** offers rewarding views and a chance to explore a distinctive alpine ecosystem along the barren, windswept ridge. The rugged hike is just over 10 miles round-trip, starting where the Appalachian Trail crosses Route 4 between Rangeley and Madrid. Be sure to bring extra clothes, since the weather can deteriorate rapidly above timberline with unpleasant consequences for the ill prepared.

The sleepy town of Rangeley, on the east shore of sparkling Rangeley Lake, has been a favorite destination for outdoorspeople for more than a century. The town's elevation is 1,546 feet, and the evening temperature often has a bit of a bite even in the midst of summer. Hunting, fishing, and canoeing remain the main allure during the warmer months, and in the winter both downhill and cross-country skiing, as well as snowmobiling and ice fishing, provide the entertainment. Travelers find a number of options for lodging and restaurants in the area, from very modern to very rustic. The chamber of commerce (864–5364) has a booth at the lakeside town park and can offer plenty of information on what's available.

One person smitten with the Rangeley region was Wilhelm Reich, a controversial scientist who had worked with Sigmund Freud. While working with Freud in Austria, Reich came to believe that Freud's theories of sexual behavior had more than an academic usefulness: They could also be applied clinically. Reich authored *The Function of the Orgasm* and attempted to cure neuroses by inducing sexual pleasure. This was controversial enough, but his theories about "orgone"—a sort of life force that he claimed could be detected, measured, and manipulated—led to a final break with Freud.

Following Hitler's rise to power, Reich lived in four countries before finally settling at Rangeley in 1942 to further his study of "orgonomy." He designed and built an angular stone house, high upon a hill overlooking the lakes, which he called **Orgonon.** With an array of peculiar-looking devices, he set about furthering his studies but failed to convince many mainstream scientists of orgonomy's validity. He also constructed something called a "cloud buster," a frightful-looking creation resembling an antiaircraft gun, which he claimed removed orgone from the atmosphere, thereby shifting the atmospheric balance and producing rain.

In 1947 the *New Republic* magazine published an article entitled "The Strange Case of Wilhelm Reich," drawing attention to Reich's claims. The article focused the unwelcome spotlight of the Food and Drug Administration on Dr. Reich, and in particular on the "orgone energy accumulators" he built at Orgonon. Patients sat in these boxlike accumulators, which were designed to absorb orgone and infuse the inhabitants with a renewed energy. The FDA accused him of fraud and took him to court. Reich paid no attention to the courts, which he maintained lacked the authority to pass judgment on scientific matters. In 1957 Reich was finally arrested after one of his students crossed state lines with an accumulator. The strange case of Wilhelm Reich ended at a federal penitentiary, where shortly after incarceration he died of heart failure at the age of sixty.

Orgonon was bequeathed to a private trust and today is managed as a memorial to Reich and his works. The building and views are visually stunning, and the fifteen-minute slide show about Reich's life offers a fascinating look at a complex mind. Many of Reich's devices are on display inside the house, as are many of the Edvard Munch-like paintings he created after he took up oil painting in 1952. A cloud buster is exhibited near a bust of the scientist a short walk from the house at an overlook with a magnificent view of Rangeley Lake.

Orgonon is open in June, July, and August Tuesday through Sunday, 1:00 to 5:00 P.M. (Open in September on Sundays only.) The hour-long tour is $3 for adults; children under twelve free. The grounds are 3.5 miles west of the town of Rangeley on Route 4. For more information call 864–3443.

Carrabassett Valley

If you've got a hankering to see a moose (most visitors to the state don't go away happy unless they've seen one), the drive from Rangeley to Stratton and onward up to Eustis is likely to deliver. This remote 25-mile route up Route 16 and continuing on Route 27 passes through prime moose habitat, with low-growing shrubs offering a tasty banquet for these herbivores. Your best bet is to head out before sunset and enjoy the drive, perhaps making your destination the attractive and popular Porter House Restaurant (no relation to the steak) in Eustis. Call for reservations, 246–7932.

Also in Eustis is a roadside historical marker overlooking the Dead River, along the route of Benedict Arnold's 1775 march toward Quebec. (For background see information on the Arnold Historical Society Museum, page 63.) At this bend in the river, the ill-starred expedition faced hurricane-force winds that toppled trees and created yet another obstacle. In the distance you can see Bigelow Mountain, named after Colonel Timothy Bigelow of Arnold's crew, who scaled the 4,150-foot peak in a vain attempt to see the lights of Quebec.

The towns along this part of Route 27 fall within the orbit of **Sugarloaf U.S.A.**, a modern, active ski area offering more than 2,800 feet of vertical drop, the largest in Maine. In summer attention shifts to golf and Sugarloaf's well-respected eighteen-hole golf course, designed by Robert Trent Jones II. The resort is concentrated around the base of the mountain and features a seven-story brick hotel, the Sugartree Health Club, and a number of condominium villages, where condos may be rented by the night or the week. For more information call 237–2000 or 800–843–5623.

Kingfield is the gateway to Sugarloaf and the Carrabasset Valley. Named after William King, Maine's first governor, Kingfield is a handsome and dignified town with a vaguely Old West feel to it, a world apart from the modern chalets of Sugarloaf. Travelers often come here for more than just the skiing: There's also the delightful One Stanley Avenue, a highly regarded restaurant in a Victorian house (265–5541), and the elegant 1908 Herbert Hotel (800–843–4372), which has been tastefully refurbished in recent years right down to moosehead, baby grand piano, and wine closet in the old walk-in phone booth. The food here is also exceptional.

Before leaving Kingfield be sure to visit the **Stanley Museum** on School Street. You've no doubt heard about the Stanley twins, F. O. and F. E., inventors of the Stanley Steamer. The twins and their five brothers and sisters were born and raised in Kingfield, and this intriguing museum is a well-designed memorial to their many talents. Even before the twins launched their automobile enterprise, they had made their fortune with inventions in the dry-plate photographic process, creating a company that was eventually purchased by George Eastman, Kodak's founder.

The museum, housed in a Georgian-style schoolhouse built with Stanley family donations in 1903, includes an informative exhibit on the family's history as well as three restored steamers. These aren't simply static museum pieces; the staff periodically takes them out for parades and other events. (The oil pans on the maple floor beneath the cars attest to their operational capabilities.) These exquisite automobiles, which had more in common with steam locomotives than with today's internal combustion engines, were first constructed as a hobby. When the Stanleys brought their car to the first New England auto show in 1898, they won both the time trials and the hill-climbing contest and received one hundred orders for their car within a week. The autos were manufactured between 1897 and 1925, reaching their pinnacle in 1906 when they set a land speed record of 127 miles per hour.

The museum, founded in 1981, also celebrates the achievements of the other Stanleys, most notably Chansonetta, the twins' younger sister, who proved herself an accomplished photographer. Her haunting portraits of rural and urban New England at the turn of the century are exceptional and have of late attracted respect and attention in the fine art world.

The Stanley Museum is open July through October Tuesday through Sunday, 1:00 to 4:00 P.M. Suggested donation is $1 for adults, 50 cents for children, and $3 per family. For more information call 265–2729.

At the northern end of the Sugarloaf universe is the town of Stratton, which offers several low-key hotels and restaurants. Among the more interesting is the **Widow's Walk,** an old, creaky bed and breakfast inn in an architecturally distinctive house built in 1892. Oramendal Blanchard, then Stratton's most prominent citizen, owned a timber mill as well as the local power and water companies; his Queen Anne-style home is notable for the curiously proportioned roof on the turret, which looks as if it were designed by a daft hatter. Inside, the six guest rooms are spartan but clean, furnished in flea market antique style. Many

Appalachian Trail hikers hitch rides to the inn from the trail crossing 5 miles south to enjoy a shower and a hearty meal before making the final push toward Mount Katahdin. Room rates are under $50 for two, including breakfast. For more information call 246–6901.

Farmington and Vicinity

Another bit of local celebrity may be found on the eastern edge of the county, in the prosperous town of Farmington. A branch of the University of Maine is located here, as is the nearby **Nordica Homestead,** birthplace of one of opera's glamorous stars. Lillian Norton was born at this modest farmhouse in 1857, then at age seven moved with her family to Boston. In the city she studied at the conservatory under John O'Neil, who rightly marked her as someone with significant talent. Following her studies she changed her name to Nordica, to reflect her northern roots, and was soon off to Europe. There she took the concert halls by storm. She became widely renowned as one of the few sopranos who could sing Wagnerian roles in tune, and she was feted by kings and presidents alike.

Well after her fame blossomed, Nordica's sisters purchased her birthplace as a birthday present to the star. Following the diva's death in 1914 (she succumbed to pneumonia while on a tour of the South Pacific), the 1840 home became a memorial to the legendary singer, and many of her possessions were shipped here. Among the interesting items in the collections are the diva's opera gowns (including a Viking-helmeted Brunhilde outfit) and numerous photos from her career. A number of gifts presented to Nordica by admirers are also displayed, including a lacquered teakwood table from the Empress of China and a garish velvet and gilded chair from Diamond Jim Brady.

The Nordica Homestead Museum is located off Routes 4 and 27, 2 miles north of Farmington. Turn right on Holley Road and continue on for 0.5 mile; the homestead is on the right. Open June 1 to Labor Day daily except Monday. Hours are 10:00 A.M. to noon and 1:00 to 5:00 P.M. Admission is $2 for adults, $1 for children. For more information call 778–2042.

And we can't leave Farmington without mentioning that it was also the home of Chester Greenwood, who in 1872 invented that humble but eminently useful bit of winter outerwear, the ear-muff—or ear protector, as he called it. The town celebrates his accomplishment each December during Chester Greenwood Day, when the earmuff-adorned citizenry assembles for considerable mirth and frivolity.

Off the Beaten Path in the Lower Kennebec Valley

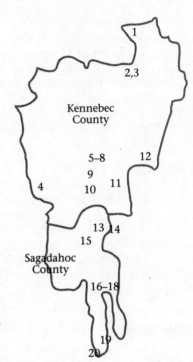

1. L.C. Bates Museum
2. Colby College
3. Railroad Cinema and Square Cafe
4. Cumston Hall
5. Maine State Museum
6. Maine State House
7. Burnsie's Homestyle Sandwiches
8. Fort Western
9. Hallowell
10. A-1 Diner
11. Arnold Historical Society Museum
12. Common Ground Fair
13. Richmond
14. Swan Island

15. Richmond Sauna and Bed and Breakfast
16. Maine Maritime Museum
17. Laughing Whale
18. Shelter Institute
19. Fort Popham
20. Hermit Island

LOWER KENNEBEC VALLEY

The Kennebec River rises at Moosehead Lake in northern Maine, then flows 150 miles to the Atlantic Ocean at Phippsburg. The river is famed for the excellent fishing and challenging white water along its northern stretches (see "North Woods"). As it descends toward the sea, the river slows and broadens, meandering through farm country and past former mill towns, trading posts, forts, and other vestiges of a varied history. The Kennebec was one of the first rivers in Maine to be explored by Europeans, who established trading routes along its length. In fact, Massachusetts' Plymouth Colony built a fur-trading post at the present site of Augusta as early as 1628. Some historians say that business was so profitable that settlers were soon able to pay off the debts incurred by the Mayflower expedition.

KENNEBEC COUNTY

Kennebec County is a rough circle in the midst of the state's southern tier. The county is some distance inland from the coast, but it can trace its history to seafaring days when lumber ships sailed up the broad river valley, providing a vital link to the world beyond. Today this gentle county offers inviting pastoral landscapes and historic riverside communities, including the state capital at Augusta.

Waterville Region

Starting upriver from Waterville, you'll find the **L. C. Bates Museum,** situated on the campus of the Hinckley School just off Route 201 south of the intersection with Route 23. The museum was founded by L. C. Bates, a successful entrepreneur from West Paris, Maine, who financed the conversion of this industrial arts building to a museum in 1924. The conversion produced eight galleries full of exhibits on natural history. The museum was operated until the late 1960s, when it fell into desuetude and was closed and locked up. In 1990 a group of local citizens banded together to reopen the museum, which had been largely undisturbed over the years save for an impressive accumulation of dust and cobwebs.

Thanks to this benign neglect, the museum was preserved in a wonderfully archaic state. The place boasts a copious collection of minerals; baskets by the Penobscot Indians; cases featuring stuffed bear, caribou, and the peculiar calico deer; and no fewer than seven magnificent mooseheads. Among the best parts of the collection are the stuffed birds—including exotic birds of paradise and the rare quetzal from Central America—displayed against outstanding impressionistic backgrounds painted by nationally known illustrator Charles D. Hubbard. Be sure also to note the massive stuffed marlin caught off Bimini by the novelist Ernest Hemingway in 1935. No one seems quite sure how it got here.

The Bates Museum is open from May 1 until the end of October on Wednesdays, Thursdays, and Fridays, 1:00 to 4:00 P.M. For more information call 872–3000.

Waterville is home to **Colby College,** just outside of town on gentle Mayflower Hill, which offers a sweeping view of the rural countryside. The campus has a staid, brick-and-ivy appearance befitting an institution of higher learning that can trace its ancestry back to 1813, when the school was founded as the Maine Literary and Theological Institution. After the Civil War it was renamed after Gardiner Colby, a Boston merchant and philanthropist, and in 1871 the college began admitting females. Although the campus has an historic and settled character, that's a bit misleading. The college moved from its original downtown site in the early 1950s, and today's classically styled buildings date from that era.

Worth visiting when you're on campus is the Bixler Art and Music Center. The art museum, housed in an open, modern wing appended to a more traditional brick structure, contains works by such Maine luminaries as Winslow Homer, John Marin, and Andrew Wyeth. Starting in 1992 the gallery will also regularly share masterpieces of the art world with the Portland Museum of Art. Exhibited for one semester every two years will be selections from the Payson collection, including works of Van Gogh, Renoir, and Degas. The museum's summer hours are Monday through Saturday 10:00 A.M. to noon and 1:00 to 4:30 P.M., and Sunday 2:00 to 4:30 P.M. Call for more information, 872–3000.

Closer to downtown Waterville, where the train tracks cross Main Street, you'll find the **Railroad Cinema and Square Cafe.** The owners have taken two good ideas—fine movies and fine foods—and combined them in one. A funky cafe occupies the spot that would be used normally for a theater lobby. The films tend toward foreign and exotic (listings may be found in the local paper), and the inexpensive dining selections feature stir-fry, pesto, and a number of sweets. Come by early for a beer and popcorn with real butter. Located at 13 Railroad Square; for more information call 873–5900.

Augusta and Environs

Performances of another sort are held in the unassuming town of Monmouth, 13 miles west of Augusta. Classic plays are performed throughout July and August by the Theater at Monmouth, a professional repertory company founded in 1970. Several plays are staged each season, and the series always includes a work or two by Shakespeare. Shows rotate each evening, offering theatergoers the option of coming back a second night for a different show. Reservations are recommended. For more information on performances, call 939–9999 Tuesday through Sunday 10:00 A.M. to 8:30 P.M.

Even if you're not much of a theater aficionado, it's worth a trip to Monmouth just to view **Cumston Hall,** the grandiose building where the plays are staged. Built in 1899–1900, this architectural flight of fancy incorporates minarets from the Middle East, Palladian windows, classical pediments, Romanesque arches and flourishes, and Victorian stained glass. Its interiors are lavishly painted with elaborate murals featuring Renaissance-style draped figures and hovering putti. In addition to the opera house, the building houses the town hall and library.

The building was designed by Harry H. Cochrane, a Monmouth resident of multiple talents. Cochrane, sometimes called the "Maine Leonardo," was an artist and muralist by training. He lacked formal education in architecture but (he told an interviewer) studied the building arts to aid his career in decorating public spaces. Cochrane went on to paint the murals in the building, design the stained glass, create the plaster ornamentation, compose the music, and conduct the orchestra for the building's opening night. Cochrane afterwards designed six other houses scattered about Monmouth, a town that displays an architecturally eclectic style. Monmouth is also home to the Monmouth Museum, a small and engaging historical museum

Cumston Hall, Monmouth

open Tuesday through Sunday 1:00 to 4:00 P.M. For more information call 933–4444.

The **Maine State Museum** in Augusta should by all accounts be on the beaten path. Surprisingly, it isn't. Few Maine residents seem to be aware of this jewel of a museum, and even fewer out-of-staters. Evidently its administrators have done a far better job in designing this thoroughly modern, informative, and appealing museum than in getting the word out.

Housed in one of those nondescript gray buildings that seem to characterize government complexes (the museum shares a roof with the Maine State Library and Archives), the collections are aesthetically arranged and neatly presented. There's a sense of discovery and exploration around each corner, from grainy film clips of early loggers working the river drives to a convincing replica of a water-driven woodworking shop. Extensive exhibits provide an overview of both the cultural and the natural history of the state—from the craft of boat building to extinction of the Eastern caribou.

One exhibit of particular interest is entitled "12,000 Years in Maine" and covers the broad sweep of Maine's earliest inhabitants. A dozen millennia ago the state's terrain more resembled the open Arctic tundra than the dense woodlands of today, and migratory native tribes passed through the region hunting caribou. Displays of artifacts found near Azichohos Lake (near Rangeley) and a full-scale diorama of a prehistoric meat cache are especially engaging. Be sure also to take the time to see the unique artifacts from the so-called Moorehead phase of Native American development (4,800 to 3,800 years ago), which are characterized by long, graceful arrowheads and adzes.

Plan to spend about two hours at the museum, which is located on the grounds of the state house complex on State Street in Augusta. Open Monday to Friday 9:00 A.M. to 5:00 P.M., Saturday 10:00 A.M. to 4:00 P.M., and Sunday 1:00 to 4:00 P.M. Admission is free. For more information call 289–2301.

Near the east end of the museum building you'll come upon a bronze statue of Samantha Smith, Maine's young "ambassador of good will." Samantha gained unexpected national and international fame after she wrote a letter to former Soviet leader Yuri Andropov questioning his commitment to peace. Andropov responded, inviting the Manchester, Maine, girl to Moscow and setting her off on an early career of diplomacy. That promising career was cut short when Samantha died in a local plane crash in 1985 at the age of thirteen. The statue captures nicely a mix of innocence and hope.

While on the state house grounds, take the time to wander around a bit to see the government in action. From the museum walk to the south entrance of the **Maine State House,** an imposing granite edifice originally designed by Charles Bulfinch, the architect of the U.S. Capitol in Washington, D.C. You can learn about the architecture and history of the building during a self-guided tour. Historical markers guide visitors from one station to the next, pointing out various clues to the building's history, such as the 1907 expansion that greatly changed its profile. If you'd like a more personal touch, pick up the marked phone inside the entrance for a free guided tour anytime between 8:30 A.M. and 4:30 P.M. Monday through Friday. The south entrance was also the former site of the state museum, as evidenced by the incongruous display cases filled with moose, deer, fish, and beaver.

From the upper floor of the state house, be sure to step out onto the open veranda, where you may see legislators and lobbyists chatting in cane-seated rockers. From this vantage you get a fine view eastward across the Kennebec River. The complex of buildings across the river is the Augusta Mental Health Institute. Directly below and across State Street is Capitol Park, where you'll find Maine's Vietnam Memorial as well as the tomb of Enoch Lincoln (a relative of Abraham), the Maine governor who moved the capital from Portland to Augusta in 1827, seven years after statehood. The park was also used as an encampment during the Civil War.

For a taste of somewhat more contemporary politics, head north to the corner of Hinchborn and State streets for a sandwich at **Burnsie's Homestyle Sandwiches** (622–6425), where famous and infamous politicos and other Augusta figures are memorialized, in a manner of speaking, with sandwiches named in their honor. There's the Governor Joe sandwich, named after former Democratic governor Joe Brennen—a standard hero loaded with salami, ham, and pepperoni. There's also the Governor Jock, named after Republican governor John McKernan, a good-looking turkey sandwich. Make of this what you will.

Across the Kennebec from downtown Augusta is **Fort Western,** a relic of the days when the river was the state's central trading route. The fort, built in 1754 by the Kennebec Proprietors (a group of major landowners), served as a garrison and supply station to protect traders venturing into the interior. The Arnold expedition passed by in 1775 en route to Quebec, but the structure was never used in combat.

Today the original 100-foot-long garrison house survives in nearly pristine condition, and the grounds have been augmented by a replica stockade fence and two blockhouses. Visitors take a self-guided walking tour, with informative history lessons offered by costumed interpreters. In the garrison house you'll see clues to the various identities the building assumed both during and after its service as a fort. The building at one time or another contained a store, officers' quarters, and other dwellings, even serving as a tenement in the 1920s. Look for intriguing bits of Americana, including an ingenious mousetrap that uses a falling block of wood to capture its prey.

Fort Western is on the east bank of the Kennebec at 16 Cony Street. Open daily mid-June through Labor Day 10:00 A.M. to 5:00 P.M. on weekdays and 1:00 to 5:00 P.M. on weekends. Open weekends only Labor Day though Columbus Day, 1:00 to 4:00 P.M. For more information call 626–2385. Admission charged.

Gardiner and Hallowell

Head 2 miles downstream from Augusta along the Kennebec's west bank (follow Route 27) and you'll pull into the quiet riverside town of **Hallowell.** Many of the younger state employees live and congregate in Hallowell, lending it a more spirited character than many Maine towns of its size. Water Street, a compact thoroughfare of stout brick buildings, offers surprisingly upscale places to dine and drink, as well as good antiques shops for browsing. Much of the nineteenth-century commercial architecture has been well preserved, and the gentrification has been subtle rather than obnoxious. Among the popular spots along Water Street are Slates, a watering hole and restaurant where you're liable to run into a state legislator or two, and the Wharf Tavern, which has an adjoining billiard hall with old-fashioned pool tables and low brass fixtures lighting the felts. Be forewarned that several used book shops in town may also require your attention, so don't plan to dash through too quickly.

In Gardiner, a few miles downstream, head for the **A-1 Diner** at 3 Bridge Street. This 1946 Worcester diner is one of those classics sought by diner fans nationwide. Inside you'll find black and white tile floors and age-burnished wooden booths, art decoish stools and neat wood trim. One aspect that's not so classic is the menu. In place of pot roast and mashed potatoes you'll find creative and delicious dishes like blue cheese meat loaf, Greek lemon soup, *pad thai,* and Siamese chicken curry. But some things don't change. You can still order tapioca pudding, served with a righteous heap of whipped cream. The A-1 (582–4804) is open breakfast through dinner every day except Sunday, when it closes at noon.

If you're an architecture buff, plan to spend some time walking off your meal by wandering Gardiner's commercial and residential neighborhoods, which have benefited recently from renovation. The Gardiner Historic District, spread along Water Street, comprises forty-seven buildings of note. Stop by either the city hall or the public library for a flyer entitled "Historic Walking Tour of Gardiner."

Gardiner was the staging point for one of the richer episodes involving the Kennebec River: the Arnold expedition in the fall of 1775. General Benedict Arnold, who was later involuntarily to lend his name as a synonym for "traitor," led one of the more tragic endeavors in the American Revolution in attempting a surprise attack on Quebec. The expedition, with about 1,150 men, endured horrendous conditions during the approach to Quebec through the Maine wilderness and failed miserably to take the city during an attack in December 1775. Arnold himself was wounded and faced misconduct charges after his return to the United States. An excellent fictional narrative dealing with the Arnold expedition may be found in Kenneth Roberts's novel, *Arundel,* which is widely available in both new and used book shops.

Learn more about the expedition at the **Arnold Historical Society Museum,** downstream from Gardiner on the river's east bank in Pittston. This fine historic home dates from 1765 and is furnished with period antiques. The Colburn family lived in the house for nearly two hundred years. Visitors get a quick education in the history of decorative arts and architecture in seeing how the house evolved over the years. Resident curator Crosby Milliman will also tell you about Major Reuben Colburn, the original resident, who hosted General Arnold and Aaron Burr for two nights while the final arrangements for the expedition were ironed out. In the barn you'll find also two early bateaux (flat-bottomed boats), which may or may not have been used in the expedition, as well as a half-dozen replicas commissioned for a 1975 reenactment.

The museum is off Route 127 in Pittston, south of Randolph and Gardiner. Open July and August weekends 10:00 A.M. to 5:00 P.M., and by appointment; call 582–7080 or 582–3648. Admission is $1.50 for adults and 50 cents for children.

Northeast of Gardiner is the Windsor County Fair Ground, home of the **Common Ground Fair,** an annual event first held in 1976 that's quickly become an enduring Maine tradition. Sponsored by the Maine Organic Farmers and Gardeners Association, the fair features craftspeople, representatives from nonprofit organizations, and organic farmers demonstrating what they do. The fairgrounds bustle and teem like any county fair, but you're more likely to see farmers with beards and ponytails than with tractor caps. There's the usual trotting out of prize vegetables and livestock as well as demonstrations of traditional New England crafts and activities, such as canoe building and horse-powered logging. Upwards of 50,000 visitors pass through the gates during the three-day event, which is held the third weekend after Labor Day.

The fairgrounds are just north of Route 17 in South Windsor. Daily admission is $4 for adults and $2 for children and elders. For more information call 623–5115.

SAGADAHOC COUNTY

With only 250 square miles, Sagadahoc is Maine's smallest county but manages to pack in a lion's share of history. Much of the state's early (and present) shipbuilding heritage can be traced here, a heritage reflected in many magnificent homes in towns and villages from Merrymeeting Bay up the Kennebec and along the lower Androscoggin River. The terrain is gentle, with thick forests opening for farmer's fields and the occasional settlement.

Richmond Area

South of Gardiner you'll come to the once-prosperous town of **Richmond,** where many sea captains settled in the years prior to the Civil War. Handsome brick buildings line the commercial streets. Elaborate Greek Revival and Italianate homes are tucked away on the side streets. Richmond has by and large been overlooked by the years; it has a slightly unkempt appearance but lends itself to fruitful explorations.

In wandering through Richmond you may find it strange to pass Saint Alexander Nevsky Church with its onion domes, or the Saint Nicholas Orthodox Parish Church, but a Russian population began settling here four decades ago. In the 1940s the town caught the attention of Vladimir Kuhn von Poushental, a Russian emigre (and former count under the czarist rulers) who found Richmond's climate and terrain much like that of Moscow. He bought up dozens of farms and buildings around Richmond, advertising parcels for sale in Russian immigrant newspapers. Transplanted Russians responded, moving in great number in the 1950s and 1960s. At the peak of the Russian influx, nearly 500 immigrants lived in this quiet riverside town, and Russian Richmond boasted its own restaurant, bootmaker, and three churches, where Russian dramas were regularly staged. Since its peak around 1970 the community has dwindled to fewer than 75. Spoken Russian may still be heard here and there from yards and open windows as you walk the peaceful streets.

Just a hundred yards or so from the Richmond town landing is **Swan Island,** a large state-owned island managed as the Steve Powell Wildlife Management Area. The island sits in the northernmost reach of Merrymeeting Bay, the largest tidal bay north of the Chesapeake. Six rivers feed into the bay, including the Kennebec and the Androscoggin, and thousands of waterfowl and other birds stop over during their spring and fall migrations along the Atlantic flyway. Species include Canada geese, teal, pintail, and the common goldeneye, among many others.

This inland bay measures some 4,500 acres, but much of the shoreline is privately owned, making a visit problematic. Swan Island offers the easiest way to have a glimpse of the bay's wildlife. The state department of inland fisheries and wildlife offers a motorboat shuttle from Richmond to the island, where limited camping is available. Access is strictly limited (remember, it's managed as a wildlife preserve), and reservations are essential. For reservations call 289–1150.

Several miles outside of town off Route 197 is the **Richmond Sauna and Bed and Breakfast,** as unusual a bed and breakfast as you'll find in Maine. Opened in 1976 by former aerospace engineer Richard Jarvi, this B&B, located on a quiet dirt road, is housed in a fine 1831 home with five guest rooms. Guests are treated like, well, guests. There's a baby grand piano in the dining room and a well-stocked library, and you're free to use the kitchen to make dinner or lunch or just to sit on the kitchen couch and chat with the other guests, who tend to be young professionals from Portland and Boston.

Although the accommodations are homey and comfortable, what really attracts people is the rustic building next door, where you'll find saunas, a hot tub, and swimming pool. Lodging prices include use of all the facilities, or if you're just passing through, you can stop by for a sauna or swim for $8 per hour. The six private saunas are wood-fired and sufficiently steamy, with the hot tub and pool just outside the door, making for a short dash in winter. Jarvi, a congenial host, has stocked a refrigerator in the waiting room with a selection of juices.

Lodging is $55 per night for a couple, $35 for a single. Sauna hours are 6:00 to 10:00 P.M. in the summer, 4:00 to 9:00 P.M. in the winter. Closed Mondays. The sauna is 1.1 miles west of I-95. Turn left on Route 138, then make the immediate left on Dingley Road. For more information call 737–4752.

Bath and Environs

Nearing the ocean, you'll come to the historic town of Bath. At the small downtown park along the Kennebec, there's a sign greeting visitors arriving by boat: "Welcome to Bath, Maine—City of Ships—Home to the Best Shipbuilders in the World." If you have arrived by boat, you're probably already aware of the city's main industry, having passed the imposing drydock of Bath Iron Works, where an Aegis class destroyer or other navy ship may be under construction or undergoing repairs. In fact, even arriving by car you may have figured out Bath's prominence: The towering red and white striped crane of the shipyard—the fourth largest in the country—dominates the landscape, providing a navigational landmark for those traveling by road and river alike.

The shipyard isn't open to the public, but you can get a good introduction to Bath's venerable shipbuilding history at the **Maine Maritime Museum** just south of Bath Iron Works. This is widely regarded as one of Maine's most informative and entertaining museums, with displays ranging from historical oil paintings of clippers and schooners to historic wooden ships moored at the museum's riverside docks. In fact, the museum is located on the former grounds of the Percy and Small Shipyard, which built forty-two schooners between 1894 and 1920. In 1909 the largest wooden ship ever built in America, the 329-foot *Wyoming*, was launched from ways that may be found in the marsh grass at the edge of the river.

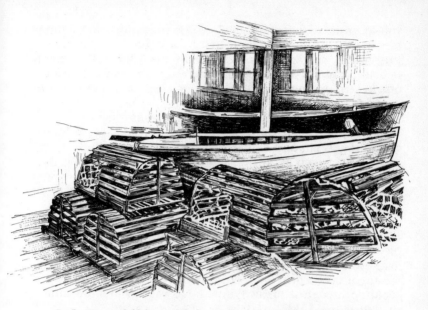

Lobster exhibit at Maine Maritime Museum, Bath

The museum is particularly strong in interpretive exhibits—such as the engaging lobstering display—which keep children intrigued and enthralled. But it's not a place for kids only. Adults who've harbored quiet fantasies of casting off lines and setting sail for points unknown will enjoy themselves at the Apprenticeshop, where boat builders employ traditional techniques in building craft sturdy enough to brave Maine's often tempestuous waters. The builders are happy to entertain any and all questions from visitors.

Museum hours are 9:30 A.M. to 5:00 P.M. daily (except Thanksgiving, Christmas, and New Year). Admission is $5.00 for adults and $2.50 for children, with discounts for seniors and families. The museum is at 243 Washington Avenue; look for blue swallowtail pennants directing the way from various points around town. For more information call 443–1316.

Bath's historic brick downtown is well worth exploring. This area has much of the charm of Portland's Old Port Exchange, but with a less aggressive quaintness. For lunch there are a number of fine eateries along Front Street and Elm Street. A walk to the top of Centre Street toward the old Sagadahoc Courthouse will bring you to Kristina's Restaurant (442–8577), housed in a pair of nine-teenth-century homes connected by a light and airy atrium. Kristina's is well known for its pecan buns, which are about as rich and dense as you'll find anywhere. Expect to wait for seating on weekend mornings, when the brunch attracts folks from Portland and beyond.

If the ship models at the maritime museum caught your eye, stop by the **Laughing Whale,** located at 147 Front Street. Owned by Kevin and Patti Butler, the shop specializes in ship model kits, which are manufactured on the premises. The shop sells forty different kits, ranging from a simple 16-inch Grand Banks dory ($33) to a 44-inch detailed fishing boat that retails for $165. Kits include blueprints, fittings, sail cloth (where appropriate), and wood. Not included in the kits are glue, paint, cutting knives, or, Kevin warns, "patience." For inspiration, fully assembled and painted models made from the kits are displayed in the showroom, which could serve as a monument to perseverance.

Laughing Whale's summer hours are 10:00 A.M. to 5:00 P.M. Monday through Saturday. Winter hours vary; call for more information at 443–5732.

For do-it-yourselfers with more ambition, a visit to the **Shelter Institute** may be in order. Located at 38 Centre Street, this nationally known school is dedicated to the proposition that anyone can build a house, cheaply and with energy-efficient materials. A basic three-week class in home design and construction demystifies the process of converting a parcel of land and some boards into a comfortable home. (An intensive two-week class is also offered.) Since Pat and Patsy Hennin founded the school in 1974, more than 10,000 people have passed through its doors. The course involves classroom study of materials and techniques, as well as trips to nearby sites to visit homes under construction. The Hennins say the class is also suitable for those wishing to renovate older homes.

The Shelter Institute's storefront, housed in an historic brick building, offers browsers an extensive line of books on home building as well as information on energy-efficient materials and building techniques. Ask to see the fifteen-minute slide show about the institute's classes. There's also an amusing display of letters the Hennins have received from around the world, often mailed to not entirely coherent addresses. (Among the more original is one directed simply to "The People Who Build Good,

Cheap Houses.") Next door is Woodbutcher Tools (442–7939), which offers a wide variety of hard-to-find woodworking tools of interest to cabinetmakers and other woodworkers. Shop hours are Monday to Friday 8:00 A.M. to 4:30 P.M., and Saturdays 9:00 A.M. to 3:00 P.M. For more information on the institute, call 442–7938.

Mouth of the Kennebec

Where the Kennebec River empties into the Atlantic, some 10 miles south of Bath, you'll find **Fort Popham,** a solid granite fortification that watches over the broad river entrance. The fort was constructed during the Civil War, when the North realized how vulnerable Bath's shipbuilding industry was to Confederate attack. The war ended before the massive 500-foot-circumference fort could be completed. Today the 30-foot walls are in good repair, and the structure is notable for its graceful stone staircases. Parking at the fort is limited. Open Memorial Day through September daily from 9:00 A.M. until sunset. Admission during summer months is $1.50 for adults and 50 cents for children under twelve.

About a half mile west of the fort is the site of the Popham Colony, or what might be called the sister city of Jamestown, Virginia. Both were established in 1607 during the first attempts by Europeans to settle the New World. Jamestown succeeded; Popham failed. About one hundred English settlers under the leadership of George Popham and Raleigh Gilbert landed here in August 1607 and constructed a fort and a storehouse. Called "Northern Virginia Colony" by the English, the settlement never took root. George Popham died during the winter, and Gilbert left for England the following spring. Disenchanted with their prospects, the remaining settlers drifted back to England the following summer, and the colony of Popham was relegated to an historical footnote.

Near the presumed site of the colony (no structures survived and few artifacts have been recovered) is Popham Beach State Park. One of the state's most popular parks, Popham provides access to a broad sweep of beach with glorious views across smaller islands offshore out toward looming Seguin Island and its doleful lighthouse. The beach parking lot fills early on pleasant weekends. A fee of $1.50 per person is charged. For more information call 389–1335.

If you're planning to camp, a spectacular private campground is located not far from Fort Popham at **Hermit Island.** Nick and Dave Sewall have owned and operated the campground since 1953, offering 275 sites (including 63 on the ocean) spread across the open, shrubby bluffs of the mile-and-a-half-long island. Access is by car along a sandy spit, and only tents and pop-up campers are allowed. Although Hermit Island has quite a few campsites, use is kept to a minimum: Only one car and two adults are allowed per site, and day visitors are not permitted. Those lucky enough to obtain a campsite (reservations are essential) have seven beaches to themselves, along with rocky bluffs and tidal pools perfect for exploring.

The island can be reached by car off Route 209 south of Bath. Open from June through mid-October. Rates range from $15 to $23 per site depending on time of year and location. For more information call 443–2101.

Off the Beaten Path on the Midcoast

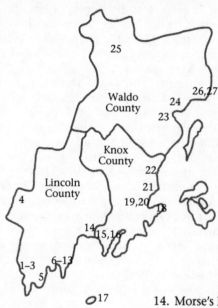

14. Morse's Kraut House
15. State Prison Store
16. Montpelier
17. Monhegan Island
18. Owls Head Transportation Museum
19. William A. Farnsworth Art Museum
20. Shore Village Museum
21. Rockport Apprenticeshop
22. Merryspring
23. Belfast and Moosehead Railroad Company
24. Perry's Nut House
25. Bryant Stove Works and Museum
26. Penobscot Marine Museum
27. Fort Knox

1. Castle Tucker
2. Musical Wonder House
3. Lincoln County Museum and Jail
4. Pownalborough Courthouse
5. Dodge Point Preserve
6. Darling Marine Center
7. Thompson Ice Harvesting Museum
8. Coveside Bar and Restaurant
9. Harrington Meeting House
10. Colonial Pemaquid
11. Pemaquid Point
12. Rachel Carson Salt Pond Preserve
13. Hog Island Audubon Camp

MIDCOAST

Traveling Maine's Midcoast presents a series of logistical challenges. Much of the coastal area between Casco Bay and Penobscot Bay is spread out on long, spindly fingers of land extending southward from Route 1. What's more, many of these fingers are separated from one another by wide rivers—such as the Kennebec, Sheepscot, and Damariscotta—that are bridged only at some distance inland. The upshot is that after you drive for miles to the tip of a peninsula, you've got to turn right around and head out the way you came in, connecting the points with stints on congested and overcommercialized Route 1.

The good news is that because these peninsulas are geographic cul-de-sacs, they maintain a sense of solitude and seclusion rare in other coastal areas. Sometimes surprisingly, old resorts and homes will be found at the tip after a long drive, traces of a time when most people traveled this coastline by water rather than land. There are oceanside farms, leafy hardwood forests, and spruce groves abutting rocky shores. Many of these desultory roads are best wandered at a slower pace than a car provides. Bicyclists almost always return enthusiastic about gently dipping and twisting roads that pass through quiet forests with periodic glimpses of a distant ocean. When the fog moves in from offshore, the views disappear but the pleasant sense of isolation is heightened.

LINCOLN COUNTY

Lincoln County extends along the coast from Wiscasset to Waldoboro, and inland to farm country around Somersville. Two major peninsulas are here: Boothbay Peninsula and Pemaquid Peninsula, both of which are blessed with at least two roads running down and back, allowing a loop tour rather than a return on the original road. The fabled rugged Maine coast may be found in spots (notably at Pemaquid Point), but for the most part it's a gentle and wooded coastline, ideal for unhurried backroad exploration.

Wiscasset Region

If you're arriving in the region via Route 1, one of the first towns you'll come to is Wiscasset, best known for two things: A pair of picturesquely decrepit schooners—the *Luther Little* and the *Hesper*—beached on the mud flats near the town landing, and the often exasperating midsummer traffic snaking its way over the Route 1 bridge across the Sheepscot River. To avoid possible midsummer frustration, plan to stop and explore for a bit in Wiscasset (which claims to be the "Prettiest Village in Maine"), then make a scenic inland detour through the quiet, historic village of Head Tide, thereby avoiding the hateful bridge.

Just a few blocks off Route 1, at the end of Wiscasset's High Street, you'll come to an imposing building known locally as **Castle Tucker.** This architecturally eccentric brick home was first built in 1807 by Judge Silas Lee, then widely modified around 1860 by Captain Richard H. Tucker, a sea captain who made his fortune in the cotton trade. Tucker added to the front of the Federal-era house a grand three-floor piazza overlooking the river, changing the home's character significantly. Among other alterations inside, he converted a dining hall into a billiards room.

The mansion is still owned by Tucker's descendants, who have opened the first floor of this unusual home to the public. A twenty-minute tour provides an intriguing look at the life of a nineteenth-century sea captain, from the paintings of great ships on the walls to the stiff, medallion-backed Victorian furniture in the parlors. Also noteworthy are architectural flourishes that include an impressive freestanding elliptical staircase, a parquet floor, and plaster trim painstakingly painted to look like oak. A clutter of curios, ranging from an egg collection in the billiard room to unusual utensils in the kitchen, allow for fine browsing.

Castle Tucker stands at the corner of Lee and High streets. Tours are offered in July and August Tuesday through Saturday 11:00 A.M. to 4:00 P.M., and by advance request in June, September, and October. Admission is $2. For more information call 882–7364.

Wrecks of *Luther Little* and *Hesper*, Wiscasset

A short stroll past the stately homes of High Street will bring you to the extraordinary museum called the **Musical Wonder House**. Here, in a rather stern 1852 house, is a mind-boggling collection of music boxes, gramophones, and player pianos from around the world. It's not the only collection of this sort in the world, but it's certainly one of the best. What's more, owner Danilo Konvalinka delights in playing the music boxes for visitors, unlike curators of other museums where the collections may be seen but not heard.

The museum, which occupies both floors of the building, starts in a grand hallway dominated by a flying staircase. Along the walls are coin-operated music boxes, mostly dating from the nineteenth century. There's no charge to wander in here and try a few boxes, or to browse in the gift shop off the back hallway. But this represents only the tip of the iceberg. Sign up for a tour and you'll have a chance to hear a sampling from among the literally hundreds of music boxes in Konvalinka's collection. The standard tour, which runs about an hour, includes the three downstairs rooms; the deluxe tour, about three hours, also includes four additional rooms upstairs.

The common conception of a music box may be of a small, square box that produces a tinkling, even tinny sound when opened. Konvalinka will put that notion to rest. His collection ranges from delicate singing-bird automatons to remarkable orchestral music boxes fully outfitted with snare drums, castanets, chimes and bells. The musical selections range from Verdi operas to Gilbert and Sullivan show tunes, with most everything in between. One of the highlights of the collection is an 1870 Girod music box from Geneva; it is the size of a small coffin and contains, among other things, a miniature reed organ. Konvalinka, an Austrian immigrant who became fascinated with music boxes at age nineteen, found this exceptional example through a classified ad and spent fifteen years restoring it. Although they represent a wide range of styles, all the music boxes share one thing in common: They produce a rich, wonderful sound that is fully absorbing.

The Musical Wonder House is at 18 High Street. Open Memorial Day to October 15 (gift shop open until Thanksgiving). Tours offered daily 10:00 A.M. to 5:00 P.M. (limited tours after Labor Day). The cost of the standard tour is $8, or two for $15 (children under twelve are $6). The deluxe tour is $25, or two for $40. Call for more information, 882–7163.

Just north of the village center on Federal Street (on the way to Head Tide), you'll pass the **Lincoln County Museum and Jail,** built in 1811 on gentle hill overlooking the river. Tours of the jail reveal dim, small cells seemingly carved out of a single block of granite—even the ceilings and floors are made of granite slabs. So it comes as something of a surprise to learn that this jail, based on plans drawn up by John Howard, an early prison reformer, was thought to represent state-of-the-art prison design. Prior to this time, most prisoners were held in large open spaces; the individual cells were thought to be a more humane approach.

The impressive stonework of the three-story jail, which was built with rock slabs ranging from 10 to 41 inches thick, is almost overshadowed by the fascinating graffiti left by early sailors, who, one presumes, were arrested for behaving like sailors. The cells range from a grim isolation cell with a narrow slit for a window to the somewhat more airy rooms on the third floor used for women, debtors, and the insane. The jail was closed in 1913, considered a relic of the past. It did have one more moment of glory before becoming a museum: During Prohibition it was used to store confiscated contraband liquor.

The tour also includes a walk through the adjoining jailer's house, where the warden and his wife lived and meals were prepared. The home features a restored kitchen and a bright exhibit area with examples of the jailer's craft, including early shackles, handcuffs, and photocopies of prison logs through which visitors are free to browse.

The Lincoln County Museum and Jail is open in July and August daily except Monday, 10:00 A.M. to 4:00 P.M. Admission is $2 for adults and $1 for children under thirteen.

Inland Lincoln County

Eight miles north of Wiscasset is the village of Head Tide. There is nothing in the way of major or minor attractions here, but the fourteen historic buildings wedged in a narrow valley along the Sheepscot make up a virtual museum of early nineteenth-century architecture. Head Tide was once a major commercial center where millers harnessed the energy from the falls at the head of the tide. Floods in 1896 and 1924 destroyed the mills and doomed the local economy. As a result, Head Tide has the feeling of having been left behind by history. The Old Head Tide Church, dating from 1838, is open to the public on Saturdays from 2:00 to 4:00 P.M. If the weather is warm, a fine swimming hole is located beneath the old milldam next to a small parking area off the road. You can return back to Route 1 via Route 194 through Alna, continuing southward on Route 215 after Route 194 ends.

En route to the Augusta area is the **Pownalborough Courthouse,** situated on the Kennebec River in the town of Dresden. This handsome 1761 building in its peaceful bucolic setting is the only remaining pre-Revolutionary courthouse in the state and one of only about a dozen nationwide. Built on the parade grounds of the 1752 Fort Shirley, the courthouse was constructed by the Kennebec Proprietors shortly after the county was incorporated. During its thirty-two years of service, the courthouse heard cases mostly involving land disputes in this remote part of the state.

After the county seat was moved and the building sold, the old courthouse served a variety of purposes but remained in the same family from 1793 to 1954, when the Lincoln County Historical Society acquired the building and seventy-five acres. Gradual restoration revealed a trove of small treasures: the original paint on the wainscoting in the tavern room; a carving of the sloop *Polly* by a British soldier who was held prisoner here during the Revolutionary War (this was plastered over and thus preserved for 150 years); and the carved initials of James Flagg, the architect's son and the courthouse's builder.

Visitors approach the courthouse down a short dirt road. A magnificent maple tree, thought to be as old as the courthouse itself, stands before this exceptionally well-proportioned building. The tour lasts between an hour and an hour and a half, depending on how many questions you muster, and includes an appealing exhibit on the once-flourishing Kennebec ice trade, when Kennebec River ice was shipped as far away as Calcutta. The courtroom proper is on the second floor and is far more spare and less grandiose than its latter-day equivalent. Perhaps the most subtle indicator of the rich era in which this building was constructed is on the third floor, where you can see a 52-inch-wide pine plank, a sign of the extraordinary bounty of the early forest.

The courthouse is east of Richmond on Route 128, 1.3 miles north of Route 197. Open in July and August Wednesday through

Saturday 10:00 A.M. to 4:00 P.M., and Sunday noon to 4:00 P.M. Tours cost $3 for adults and $1 for children under thirteen. For more information call 882–6817.

Boothbay Peninsula

The Boothbay peninsula between the Sheepscot and Damariscotta rivers is one of the major stops on the contemporary tourist's pilgrimage along the Maine coast (the others include Camden and Acadia National Park). As such, the town of Boothbay Harbor is often inundated with travelers—and has been since the 1870s, when steamer service to Bath was established. Parking is tight and the shops tend to reflect the interests of tourists more than of typical Mainers. If time is an issue, I would recommend bypassing the Boothbay peninsula in favor of the Pemaquid peninsula, farther east, which to my mind has more drama, intrigue, and history.

If you have time for both peninsulas, be sure to sample one of the boat tours out of Boothbay Harbor, with cruises ranging from a short tour of the harbor to day-long trips to Monhegan Island. Whale watches and puffin cruises are also an option, as are deep-sea fishing trips. Tours are plentiful—more than twenty tour boats are berthed in the harbor—and prices range from $5 to $25. Wander along the waterfront to peruse brochures and discuss options with tour boat captains.

If you're in the mood for a pleasant woodland walk, plan to stop at the **Dodge Point Preserve** on the northeast side of the peninsula just south of Newcastle. This attractive riverside parcel of land was recently acquired by the Damariscotta River Association and the Land for Maine's Future board and is open to the public for quiet recreation. A peaceful lane runs in a loop around the property, past vast stands of red pine, along a pond and marsh, beside stone walls, and beneath towering oaks. The entire loop may be hiked in about an hour; add more time if you stop for a swim at Sand Beach along the tidal river.

The preserve is located slightly over a mile south of the town of Newcastle. Look carefully for a small sign reading "FL 30" (fire lane 30) on the east side of the road. The fire road is gated; park alongside River Road. A crude map is posted near the gate to enable visitors to get their bearings. Open daylight hours. No camping.

Pemaquid Peninsula

The Pemaquid peninsula is a long wedge driven into the Gulf of Maine between Johns and Muscongus bays. From the attractive river town of Damariscotta to bold Pemaquid Point, the entire peninsula is well worth exploring at a leisurely pace. Stop to enjoy the historic buildings, investigate tide pools, or have a lobster along the ocean's edge. Take the time to explore both arms of this peninsula, Pemaquid Point itself and Christmas Cove.

For background on the marine life of the region and some insight into the marine research that's underway in the state, plan to visit the **Darling Marine Center** in Walpole. Located at the end of a winding drive shaded by pines, this pleasing compound is administered as a research center by the University of Maine. (The somewhat ungainly formal name is Ira C. Darling Center for Research, Teaching and Service.) The campus hosts academic researchers under the guidance of about a dozen faculty members. Most of the buildings are clustered around the upper campus; be sure to wander down about a half mile to the lower campus to see the new flowing seawater facility, which opened in 1991.

Visitors are welcome to the campus during research hours. Guided tours are offered during the summer, Monday through Friday 9:00 A.M. to 4:00 P.M. For more information call 563–3146. The center is located off Route 129 on the way to Christmas Cove. Turn right after passing the golf course; the center's driveway is 1 mile on the right.

Just north of South Bristol, a pleasantly unadorned fishing village, you'll pass the **Thompson Ice Harvesting Museum** on the east side of the road. An icehouse has been located here for decades; the present icehouse was built in 1990, modeled after one that previously stood at the site. The museum is on land donated by the Thompsons and operated by volunteers who feared that this window on history would be closed forever.

This modest museum isn't merely an historic display; it's an operating icehouse. Each winter, generally in February, community members assemble on the ice pond and use old tools to harvest the ice. First the workers score the pond's surface into blocks of 20 inches by 30 inches. With both machine and hand saws, they then cut out the blocks along the scoring and clear a "canal" the length of the pond. They then float the foot-thick ice blocks along using pick poles and ice tongs, load them onto a massive conveyer, and transfer them into the shed, whose walls are packed with 10 inches of sawdust insulation. The 7-foot-high pile of ice is then topped with an insulating layer of hay and sealed up to wait for summer sales.

If you visit in summer, there's little activity but plenty of information. A shed adjoining the storage room displays tools of the trade, and an outdoor display features photos of the ice-harvesting operation. Visitors can scramble up a ladder to look down on the blocks of ice glistening through the hay. The ice is sold throughout the summer to local fishermen, who use it to keep their catch fresh.

The Thompson Ice Harvesting Museum is on Route 129 north of South Bristol. Open in July and August Wednesday, Friday, and Saturday 1:00 to 4:00 P.M., or by appointment anytime between mid-June and mid-October. The suggested donation is $1 for adults and 50 cents for children. For more information, or to schedule an appointment, call 644–8551.

The best way to see the Maine coast is by yacht, preferably a very large and expensive one. If such an endeavor is out of your budget, a cheaper way to live out a Walter Mitty-style fantasy is to head to the **Coveside Bar and Restaurant** at Christmas Cove, which was named by explorer John Smith, who is said to have anchored here on Christmas Day in 1614. It's well off the beaten path for those traveling by car but a convenient and well-protected harbor for those cruising by boat. The food at the Coveside isn't all that distinguished, but the atmosphere more than makes up for it. The restaurant overlooks the scenic harbor, and yacht flags from around the world hang from the bar's wall like an unruly shag carpet. Large and impeccably maintained yachts are often moored near the docks, and regular visitors include such illustrious yachtsmen as Walter Cronkite and William F. Buckley. If you've got the time, ask the bartender to tell the story about the suede shoes above the bar, which once belonged to a notably obnoxious Wall Street tycoon who served time in jail.

The fastest and best way to cross from Christmas Cove to Pemaquid Point is by way of Old Harrington Road. Along the way, stop at the spare and handsome **Harrington Meeting House,** one of three meetinghouses built in the area in 1772.

(Only one other remains: the Old Walpole Meeting House off Route 129, where services are held at 3:00 P.M. each Sunday throughout the summer.) The Harrington Meeting House, located between two cemeteries with a view to the harbor beyond, was meticulously restored between 1960 and 1967. The interior is austere yet elegant, built with massive hand-hewn timbers and an extraordinary eye for proportion and form. An intricately carved pulpit looks out over the box pews. The second-floor galleries were left open to allow for a small museum, which displays arrowheads, portraits of local personalities, and a collection of photographs of early twentieth-century ships.

The meetinghouse is open July and August, Monday, Wednesday, Friday, and Saturday afternoons 2:00 to 4:30 P.M. No admission is charged, but donations are gratefully accepted.

Farther down the peninsula is **Colonial Pemaquid,** the site of one of Maine's earlier settlements, circa 1625. Since 1965 excavations have been ongoing here, the earth gradually yielding up clues about this village and its settlers, who endured many years of privation as well as attack from the French and Indians. Colonial Pemaquid is today maintained by the state. Excavations pock the broad, grassy field overlooking Pemaquid River and Johns Bay, and a small museum on the grounds displays artifacts uncovered during the digs. Abundant historical markers help make sense of the holes, where visitors may view stone foundations of former barracks.

The centerpiece of the park is Fort William Henry, a 1907 replica of a massive stone fort built on the point in 1692. One of many constructed on the site from 1630 onward, this was one of the earliest stone forts constructed in the United States and was widely thought to be impregnable. Such hopes were soon put to rest; the fort was rather easily destroyed by the French led by Baron de Castin, after whom was named the east Penobscot Bay town of Castine. The fort is open to the public and offers fine views across the waters. Next door is an old captain's house, built in 1790, which is closed to the public.

Colonial Pemaquid is open from the end of May until Labor Day daily 9:30 A.M. to 5:30 P.M. Admission is $1.50 for adults and 50 cents for children; this includes both the museum and the fort. The restoration is located west of the town of New Harbor. Turn right off Route 130 just south of the intersection with Route 32.

Continuing south on Route 130 will bring you to dramatic, windswept **Pemaquid Point**. Near the tip is the scenic Pemaquid Lighthouse, built in 1827 and visible on a clear night 14 miles to sea. Although the point is a popular destination, visitors always sense an air of remoteness and foreboding, even when they share the experience with a number of other people. Pemaquid Point is quintessential Maine coast, particularly when a storm churns the sea and sends waves exploding up the fissures in the rocky point.

Inside the former lightkeeper's house is the Fisherman's Museum, filled with all sorts of information and exhibits relating to the sea. There's an informative map showing the sixty-one lighthouses of Maine; displays of netting, traps, and buoys; and a monumental twenty-eight-pound lobster, which, somewhat disappointingly, was caught off Rhode Island. Be sure to take time to wander through the museum and the nearby gallery featuring works of local artists—although the real draw is the smell of the salt air and the surge of the surf. The museum is open daily 10:00 A.M. to 5:00 P.M., except Sunday when hours are 11:00 A.M. to 5:00 P.M.

Heading back up the east side of the peninsula on Route 32, you'll pass by the harbor that lends New Harbor its name. One of the better lobster pounds in the state may be found here at Shaw's (677-2200), where you can enjoy a crustacean while watching the lobster boats come and go through the narrow inlet that provides access to the open sea.

The **Rachel Carson Salt Pond Preserve** is a short drive north on Route 32. Plan to arrive at low tide, when the seas have receded to leave a quarter-acre tidal salt pond in a broad cobblestone cove. The pond is perfect for exploring marine life, as author and naturalist Rachel Carson discovered during hours spent here collecting information for her best-selling book *The Edge of the Sea*. The preserve, which is owned and managed by the Nature Conservancy, was dedicated to Carson in 1970. Look for starfish and green sea urchins, and dig through the seaweed for blue mussels, green crabs, and periwinkles. A brochure describing some of the indigenous marine life may be picked up at the registration box. Some seventy wooded acres across the road are also owned by the Nature Conservancy and are open to walking during daylight hours.

If you'd like to be better informed about the wildlife you're seeing, either on land or in the tide pools, consider signing up for one of the week-long classes at **Hog Island Audubon Camp,** located just off Keene Neck south of Medomak. Six-day sessions focusing on field ornithology and marine biology are offered throughout the summer, with adult "campers" living in rustic housing at the 333-acre island wildlife sanctuary. (Write in advance for upcoming classes and costs: National Audubon Society, 613 Riversville Road, Greenwich, CT 06831.) Visitors are welcome to walk the trails on the island, but there's a catch: You've got to provide your own transportation across about 150 yards of water from Hockomock Point. The Audubon motorboat shuttle is for program participants only. There's another option: Audubon's mainland headquarters offers a mile-long nature trail with classic Maine views down island-filled Muscongus Bay. Stop by the office and ask for a nature trail guide, then spend an hour or so exploring Hockomock Trail, reading about forest and field ecology as you walk along. To reach the trail, look for Keene's Neck Road off Route 32 about 5 miles north of Round Pond. Drive to the end and follow signs for visitors' parking.

Waldoboro and Vicinity

Back along Route 1 in Waldoboro, lunch at Moody's Diner (832–7468) might be in order. If Maine decided to establish an official Maine State Restaurant, Moody's would be a strong contender. The diner has been a popular destination among tourists and truckers for decades and serves heaping portions at reasonable prices. Don't gorge too excessively on the main course, since you'll be needing to leave room for some of Moody's famous cream pies. Open twenty-four hours, except midnight to 5:00 A.M. on Fridays and Saturdays.

Native food of another sort may be found on a pleasant drive north of Route 1 in North Waldoboro. **Morse's Kraut House** can trace its roots back to 1910, when Virgil Morse began making sauerkraut in his basement for descendants of the German immigrants who had settled in Waldoboro's environs. "Old Verge," as he was known, made a tart and tangy kraut that was widely popular and available in local stores. After Virgil's death in 1963, his son and his widow ran the business until finally selling it in 1988.

New owner Tom Cockroft, a Maine native, is dedicated to keeping the Morse tradition alive. He grows his own cabbage on four acres across the road, and he produces some seventy tons of fresh sauerkraut each year. "I like to keep it white and crunchy," he says, and he's been successful at it, using a ninety-year-old recipe that calls for less salt than the industry standard. The cabbage is entirely hand cut; then Cockroft hand packs it in plastic barrels using a wooden mallet. Visitors can watch the kraut process during cool weather—Cockroft generally starts making it around the last week in August, continuing through early June. If you're here in midsummer, you can still stop by to purchase a jar, or to have fresh kraut on a bratwurst or a Reuben. Several picnic tables are located on a rise next to the barn, offering open views across cabbage fields to Medomak Pond.

Morse's Kraut House is 7.6 miles north of Route 1 on Route 220. Open year-round Monday through Friday 8:00 A.M. to 7:00 P.M., and Saturdays and Sundays 10:00 A.M. to 7:00 P.M. For more information call 832–5569.

KNOX COUNTY

Named after Revolutionary War officer Henry Knox, one of the area's chief proponents and earliest developers (see Montpelier, below), Knox County contains some of Maine's highly popular coastal destinations, including Camden and the islands off Rockland. I also include Monhegan Island here, even though Monhegan is actually in Lincoln County, since access is commonly from Port Clyde on the St. George peninsula. As with much of Maine, the inland townships contain mostly small farms and villages with little in the way of attractions but with plenty of peaceableness and charm.

Thomaston and Environs

The hospitable and historic town of Thomaston is dominated at either end by two imposing structures: a cement factory on the east side (formerly owned by the Passamaquoddy Indians), and the gray and vaguely sinister Maine State Prison on the west side. One of the more unusual gift shops in the state is adjacent to the prison on Thomaston's main street: the **State Prison Store.** Inside you'll find a variety of items made (or at least assembled) by the inmates. These range from ashtrays made from Maine license plates to lobster trap tables, cedar boxes, and simple pine furniture. Not everything is made by the inmates; look for a tag or stamp on the bottom reading: "Made by Inmate. Maine State Prison." Items for sale are mostly of wood, but some leatherwork and fabric is also represented. The cash register is staffed by uniformed prison officials, who informed me that shoplifting was a problem here like everywhere else. Open daily 9:00 A.M. to 7:00 P.M.

Just east of the Thomaston center, at the intersection of Routes 1 and 131, you'll see a massive Federal home set on a hillside. This is **Montpelier,** home of Henry Knox, Revolutionary War major general, first secretary of war, and one of Maine's principal landowners during the early days of the republic. (Knox came into his vast landholdings largely through a fortunate marriage.) Seeking to build a country estate not unlike Washington's Mount Vernon or Jefferson's Monticello, Knox set about building Mont-

Montpelier, Thomaston

pelier in 1793. The grand plan ended as a dismal failure. The Maine winters were ill suited to a house of this scale, and Knox proved to be a less-than-shrewd businessman, quickly dissipating his fortune. Montpelier was constructed but never established roots.

The present building is actually a replica, built during the Great Depression, and is not on the original site. The original home overlooked the St. George River and was demolished in 1871 to make way for the railroad. Other than a pair of supporting walls added on the second floor, the present Montpelier is a faithful reproduction of the original. Maintained and operated by the state, the home is also furnished with many items from the original homestead.

Tours run about forty-five minutes and include both floors of this sprawling mansion. Among the architectural elements that distinguish the building are the graceful oval front room, the semi-flying double staircase (also referred to as a "butterfly staircase"), and clerestory windows high above the hallway. Note the detailing throughout, including wallpaper reproduced from scraps of the original, and the intricately carved moldings throughout the house. Much of the mansion has suffered from neglect and deterioration over the years thanks to declining state budgets, but the magisterial form and many classical elements shine through.

Montpelier is open between Memorial Day and Labor Day Wednesday through Sunday 9:00 A.M. to 5:30 P.M. Admission is $2 for adults and 50 cents for children under twelve. For more information call 354–8062.

St. George Peninsula

Turning south on Route 131, you'll pass a few small fishing towns and soon reach the working waterfront at Port Clyde, the traditional departure point for Monhegan Island. (Island excursions are also available from Boothbay Harbor and New Harbor.) Even if you don't have time to visit the island, Port Clyde is worth the drive. It's a town of weatherbeaten clapboards and worn shingles, clinging to a point seemingly at the edge of the earth. Stop for lunch at either the Dip Net or the Port Clyde General Store, both of which share a deck overlooking the harbor.

The general store seems right out of a Sarah Orne Jewett tale, with creaky floorboards and a cracker-barrel atmosphere. A deli counter in the back offers sandwiches and pizza. Scattered around the deck are lumber, propane tanks, and other items destined for the islands hereabouts.

Access to **Monhegan Island** is via the *Laura B.,* a sturdy boat operated by Captain James Barstow with three departures daily in midsummer (fewer trips the rest of the year). The 12-mile trip takes one hour and ten minutes. The boat passes several inshore islands before making the open-sea crossing to the misty pale blue knob of Monhegan. Reservations (372–8848) are encouraged. The round-trip fare is $20 for adults and $14 for children. Parking at Port Clyde is an additional $3 per day.

It's clearly more than coincidence that artists have flourished on 700-acre Monhegan Island and have been attracted to its distant shores for decades. Rockwell Kent and George Bellows both spent time on Monhegan; Jamie Wyeth still summers here and can sometime be seen painting in an up-ended wooden crate (to keep tourists from looking over his shoulder as he works). The island is imbued with a stark natural drama and has a thin, almost arctic light. The architectural style is also unique, putting its own island twist on the traditional Maine vernacular. In recent years the island has become somewhat inundated with day trippers who spend an hour or two wandering about before returning back to the mainland. The number of overnight accommodations has held steady, however, and seems about the right carrying capacity for the island. To get a real sense of the place, plan to spend at least one night. You'll be doing yourself an injustice otherwise.

Monhegan has three inns, only one of which—the Island Inn—has its own generator and electric lights. The other two, as well as the few bed and breakfasts, provide kerosene lamps. Guests are advised to bring flashlights. Reservations are essential during the peak months of July and August; write or call for details. Addresses are the same for all: Monhegan Island, ME 04852. The Island Inn (596–0371) is the largest of the bunch, with six of its rooms featuring private baths. The Monhegan House (594–7983) is rambling and picturesque. The Trailing Yew (596–0440) has rooms spread about a compound of four buildings, most offering views of the ocean. Family-style meals are served in the main building.

Be sure to bring hiking boots or sturdy shoes, since walking is the thing. About two-thirds of the island is undeveloped, ranging from dense, quiet forests to open meadows atop dramatic headlands. If you're spending the night, you'll have time to walk the Cliff Trail around the island's perimeter as well as explore some of the inland trails, such as the peaceful Cathedral Woods Trail, where children often build miniature "fairy houses" of twigs and moss. There's a small museum of local culture next to the lighthouse; guests tend to gather here late in the day to watch the sun sink over Manana Island.

Rockland Area

Back on the mainland, continue eastward up the coast from Port Clyde. You'll soon make this discovery: You're actually heading more northward than eastward. That's because of Penobscot Bay, a massive indentation in the Maine coast extending about 50 miles from Port Clyde to Bucksport. Three major islands with year-round communities are located in the bay, along with dozens of smaller, uninhabited islands. Following Route 1 along the western edge of the bay affords occasional views, but, as always, you'll get a better sense of the area if you leave the security of the main highway and venture on the smaller byways.

From the attractive and still-bustling seaport town of Rockland, make a detour to the **Owls Head Transportation Museum,** another one of those attractions that sounds deadly dull but turns out to be quite fascinating.

Housed in a series of multicolored hangars at one end of the regional airport, the cavernous, 65,000-square-foot exhibit space is filled with an array of automobiles, planes, bicycles, and motorcycles, many of which show an attention to aesthetics that seems long since abandoned by more modern designers. The collection ranges from a 1910 Harley Davidson motorcycle ("does the work of three horses," claimed the advertisement) to a 1929 Rolls Royce Phantom 1 Tourer. There's also a replica of a 1911 Burgess-Wright Model F, the Wright Brothers' first production plane. For the more mechanically inclined, there's a room called the Engineerium, displaying the museum's impressive collection of internal combustion engines.

Most Maine museums are best visited on weekdays, when the crowds are thinnest. That's not the best advice for Owls Head; special events are usually scheduled for Saturdays and Sundays in the summer, during which the fine museum pieces are brought out of the hangar and taken for a ride or flight. The museum's collections are often joined by other privately owned museum-quality pieces that are driven or flown in for the event.

The museum is 2.8 miles south of Rockland on Route 73. Open year-round. May through October open daily 10:00 A.M. to 5:00 P.M.; November through April open weekdays only. Admission is $4 for adults, $2.50 for children under twelve, with a maximum of $12 per family. For more information call 594–4418.

When in Rockland visit the **William A. Farnsworth Art Museum.** One of the state's finest museums, the Farnsworth was established in 1935 when the notably eccentric and reclusive Lucy Farnsworth died at the age of ninety-six, bequeathing her estate of more than $1 million to endow a museum in her father's memory. The museum contains a superb selection of American impressionists, including Childe Hassam, Maurice Prendergast, and Josephine Miles Lewis (also distinguished as the first woman to graduate from Yale University). Many of the Monhegan artists are also featured here, among them Rockwell Kent, George Bellows, and Robert Henri. The museum is perhaps best known for its Wyeth collection with works from all three generations: N. C., Andrew, and Jamie. The museum also has an extensive collection of works by Rockland native and internationally acclaimed sculptor Louise Nevelson. Next door is the Farnsworth Homestead, the house where Lucy Farnsworth lived and died. It's open throughout the summer and has been preserved to show a typical Victorian home.

The museum is in downtown Rockland at 19 Elm Street, between the north- and southbound legs of Route 1. Open year-round. June through September, open 10:00 A.M. to 5:00 P.M. daily except on Sundays, when hours are 1:00 to 5:00 P.M. Closed Mondays throughout the rest of the year. Admission is $3 for adults, $2 for students through high school, and free to children under twelve. For more information call 596–6457.

Just a few blocks away is the **Shore Village Museum,** an ample and intriguing collection of lighthouse-related items and nautical gear. Anyone remotely curious about the history of lighthouses should visit, as, for that matter, should those who have never given lighthouses a second thought. This rambling building, which also houses a collection of Civil War memorabilia from Rockland's Old Grand Army building, features several rooms filled with lighthouse artifacts, including the largest collection of lighthouse lenses in the United States. Dominating the collection is a spectacular 9-foot-tall lighthouse lens from Boothbay Harbor dating from 1855. The light amplification is extraordinary, answering the rarely asked question of how lighthouses worked before electricity. Throughout the two floors of exhibits you'll also find early navigational gear, compasses, fog detectors, and myriad other items that helped sailors get from one point to another without running afoul of the rocks.

The museum is located at 104 Limerock Street in Rockland. Open June 1 to October 15 daily 10:00 A.M. to 4:00 P.M. Admission is free, but donations are encouraged. For more information call 594–4950.

In Rockland you'll also find the terminal of the state ferry line that services the large Penobscot Bay islands of North Haven and Vinalhaven. Both have year-round communities, but Vinalhaven tends to harbor more fishermen and be a bit more earthy than old-money North Haven. Vinalhaven is also a bit more accommodating to tourists, offering overnight accommodations in several B&Bs and inns; North Haven's one inn closed in 1991 but may reopen if a new buyer is found (check at 867–2219). Both islands have paved roads winding through forest and field, affording outstanding views of the ocean and offshore islands. If you're disinclined to bike, mopeds may be rented on Vinalhaven. The ferry schedule varies throughout the year; call for current information, 596–2202.

In addition to the ferries, one of the larger windjammer fleets in the world is based on Rockland's no-nonsense industrial waterfront and offers trips that range from an afternoon to a week. The wooden ships with their towering masts are an impressive sight tied up at dock, but you need to experience these ships under sail to appreciate them fully. Overnight accommodations aboard vary from the cramped to the luxurious. If asked, most captains are forthright about what they offer—nothing makes for a longer summer than trying to cheer up disgruntled customers.

Rates for a week's worth of windjamming run somewhat less than $100 per day per person, including all meals. Shorter trips are slightly higher priced. Your best bet for scheduling a wind-jammer vacation is to contact the Maine Windjammer Association for information well in advance of your trip (P.O. Box 317, Rockport, ME 04856; 800–624–6380). If you're already in Rockland and would like to check to see if anything's available, stop by the Rockland Chamber of Commerce office at the public landing, where windjammer brochures are distributed. Windjammer cruises are also available out of Camden and Rockport.

Camden and Rockport

The harbor town of Rockport has a more genteel and yachty feel to it than Rockland to the south. The harbor is smaller and more scenic; attractive homes and estates cluster along the flanking hills. Along the harbor just south of the center of town is the **Rockport Apprenticeshop,** dedicated to preserving the craft of fine wooden boat building. At any given time up to fourteen apprentices are working with master builders to construct boats ranging from a 9-foot skiff to a 37-foot Friendship sloop. All potential apprentices must first participate in a six-week intern-ship, building one of the shop's well-known Susan skiffs, after which they are invited to apply for an apprenticeship. The non-profit apprentice program, which was spun off in 1982 from the Maine Maritime Museum in Bath, serves admirably in bridging the gap between past and present.

Visitors are invited to view ongoing boat work from an open loft above the shop floor, where two or three boats are under construction. A volunteer is usually available to answer questions or to provide information on the apprentice program. Short classes are also offered, with instruction ranging from wood carving to tips on what to look for when buying a boat.

The Rockport Apprenticeshop is off Elm Street on the south side of the harbor. The visitor's loft is open daily 10:00 A.M. to 5:00 P.M. A donation of $2 is suggested. For more information call 236–6071.

When John Smith sailed the coast in 1605, he noted "the high mountains of the Penobscot, against whose feet the sea doth beat." In later years the town of Camden flourished here, attracting fishermen and the wealthy, both of whom saw the advantages in the well-protected harbor. For a long time Camden was something of a secret, a gem hidden between mountains and sea.

Camden is no longer a secret. It's been discovered by just about every traveler to Maine, including tour bus operators. Change has come over the years, and not always for the better. Camden isn't yet as kitschy as Boothbay Harbor or Bar Harbor, but it appears to be well on its way. Nonetheless, a number of elegant inns dot the hillsides around the harbor, and Camden also boasts some excellent restaurants and shops. A walk around town should include the attractive town park, designed near the turn of the century by the firm of Frederick Law Olmsted, the designer of Central Park. The park offers an excellent view of the harbor, which throughout the summer is packed tightly with tall-masted sailing ships and all other manner of watercraft.

An oasis of serenity amid Camden's commotion may be found just off Route 1 south of town. **Merryspring** is a sixty-six-acre floral preserve dedicated to the planting and preservation of Maine flowers and shrubs. Although barely a third of a mile from the highway, it's well off the tourist track; if anyone's here when you visit, it's almost sure to be a local gardener or volunteer. An information kiosk near the parking area has maps for the taking. A couple of miles of trails meander through a variety of terrain, with pleasing views of the surrounding Camden Hills. Don't miss the extensive and exuberant herb garden near the entrance, featuring medicinal, culinary, and medieval herbs. The park is open daily year-round from dawn to dusk, and no admission is charged. From Route 1, turn west on Conway Road near the Bass Shoe Outlet.

Two of the most prominent of the Camden Hills are located within 6,500-acre Camden Hills State Park: Mount Battie and Mount Megunticook. Battie's 800-foot summit is accessible by car up a short toll road, as well as by foot trail. On the summit is a plaque commemorating one of Camden's most illustrious residents, the poet Edna St. Vincent Millay. The ledges on the southeast face of Mount Megunticook are accessible via a forty-minute hike up a well-marked but rocky 1-mile trail. From either Battie or Megunticook, outstanding views of Penobscot Bay lie before you, including the island of Vinalhaven and the open ocean beyond. Try to arrive at one of the peaks early in the morning, before the crowds ascend, when you can enjoy the sun glinting through the mist on the ocean's surface.

WALDO COUNTY

Founded in 1827, shortly after statehood, Waldo County includes the northeast part of Penobscot Bay. Renowned as a major poultry region earlier in this century, the county now relies more on small businesses and tourism. It also seems to be attracting more artists each year to its pleasant communities, in particular to the county seat at Belfast.

Belfast and Vicinity

The town of Belfast was first settled by Scotch-Irish settlers in 1770, then went through a series of economic booms and busts related to shipbuilding and the poultry industry. In recent years it's found a fair degree of prosperity as a haven for artists, who live along the coast and in the nearby hills. Their work may be found in several galleries in downtown Belfast—which consists of two commercial streets, one paralleling the harbor a hundred yards above it, and one descending to the water's edge. Many fine Federal and Greek Revival homes line the residential streets nearby.

Near the waterfront you'll find the terminus of the **Belfast and Moosehead Railroad Company.** Sometimes called the "Broken and Mended," the B&M had the distinction until recently of being the oldest city-owned railway in the nation. The town sold the line and the equipment in 1991, but the new owner has declared his intention of keeping it up and running, offering hour-and-a-half passenger tours to the village of Brooks and back. The trips depart from an 1870s freight building amid a weed-choked railyard. Passengers travel in coaches dating from the 1920s through the 1940s, pulled by a diesel engine. The route passes along a river, then through forest and field to Brooks, where passengers disembark to explore the restored railroad station. Not to spoil the surprise, but the trip also involves a holdup by some rather unsavory-appearing desperadoes, an event that seems to delight more than frighten most children.

Two trains depart Belfast daily. The fare is $10 for adults and $7.50 for children. The depot is on Front Street, just north of Main Street near the town landing. Schedules and rates are subject to change; for more information call 338–2330.

Just north of Belfast on Route 1, you'll pass a landmark of sorts from Maine's early days as a tourist destination. **Perry's Nut House** (338–1630) was founded in the 1920s and has maintained much of its character over the years. It's an unadorned and forthright Tourist Trap in the finest sense, boasting a "world famous nut museum" and a display of stuffed animals from around the world. Inside the slightly dilapidated house, you'll find the usual aromatic products hawked to travelers since time immemorial (bayberry candles, cedar boxes), along with humorous hats and beaded belts. The nut museum itself may be found in a small room in the back, with exhibits ranging from the common black walnut to the Egyptian hypaene nut. There are also photographic displays along the lines of "shipping filberts to market." The stuffed animals, which are in less than pristine condition, are housed upstairs in a cramped room whose floor is not precisely level. Of course, Perry's also sells nuts, and plenty of them.

Inland Waldo County

Some miles inland, amid rolling hills and open fields, head to the small town of Thorndike. There's not much to visit except for the **Bryant Stove Works and Museum,** a collection of antique wood stoves from a wide variety of manufacturers. Most are for sale, but even if you're not in the market it's worth a stop to view these impressive icons from an earlier era.

Most of the stoves are of heavy cast iron, and many feature brilliant nickel trim polished to a high luster. All of the stoves have been meticulously restored, with the bodies sandblasted and the damaged parts replaced. Small parlor stoves and massive kitchen stoves are featured in the collection, including several white enamel stoves dating from the 1920s and 1930s. Among stoves typically on display are the massive Queen Atlantic (made by Maine's Portland Stove Foundry), the Glenwood N, and the heavily nickeled Our Clarion, made in 1880s by the Wood and Bishop Company of Bangor. Somewhat incongruously, the Bryants also sell and service player pianos, featuring a variety of pianos and a wide selection of roll music.

The Bryant Stove Works is open year-round Monday through Saturday 7:30 A.M. to 5:00 P.M., and by appointment on Sunday. For more information call 568–3665.

Northern Penobscot Bay

Passing through Searsport on Route 1, you'll see an attractive complex of white clapboard and brick buildings on the north side of the highway. Stop here. Inside these buildings are some of the most intriguing nautical items anywhere in the state. The **Penobscot Marine Museum** has been somewhat eclipsed in recent years by the rapid growth of the Maine Maritime Museum in Bath, but this extensive collection still has the power to enchant. Like Bath, Searsport was an important shipping town, launching more than three thousand vessels between 1770 and 1920 and home to 286 ship captains in the nineteenth century. The ships and captains are long gone, but ample evidence of their existence may be found at the museum. The museum unfolds in room after room, revealing its treasures slowly and pleasurably.

Well-presented exhibits throughout the museum complex inform visitors about trade routes, ship design, and the sailor's life. The Douglas and Margaret Carver Gallery contains one of the finest collection of marine paintings in the state; there's also an extensive display of chinaware and lacquered tables brought back from trading missions to the Far East. A portrait gallery highlights the classic weathered faces of the ship captains who sailed from Searsport. Two unusual exhibits include the whaling room with its centerpiece four-panel Dutch painting of whaling in the Arctic (formerly in Hearst's San Simeon), and rare scenes by accomplished amateur photographer Ruth Montgomery, who accompanied her father on a sailing trip to Argentina aboard the Portland bark *Carrie Winslow* in 1902. Montgomery deftly captured the joys and hardships of life at sea through her lens.

The Penobscot Marine Museum is open daily Memorial Day to mid-October, Monday through Saturday 9:30 A.M. to 5:00 P.M.; Sunday 1:00 to 5:00 P.M. Admission is $4 for adults, $1.50 for children under fifteen. For more information call 548–2529.

Fort Knox, on the Penobscot River across from the mill town of Bucksport, is not to be confused with the place where government gold bullion is stashed. But it is well worth exploring, particularly if you're traveling with children. This massive fort seems a valiant exercise in overkill, even considering the strategic importance of the river. Started in the 1840s, the fort was manned during the Civil War and the Spanish-American War but was never attacked. Perhaps with good reason. Visitors today can marvel at the extensive earthworks and sheer granite walls sited dramatically on a bluff overlooking the Penobscot's narrows at Verona Island. The fort is a sprawling labyrinth, full of dim hallways, irregular courtyards, wondrous angles, and echoes that fascinate children endlessly. Much of the masonry work is exceptional, particularly the graceful spiral staircases of hewn granite. In an inspired marriage of art and architecture, *Macbeth* was staged here for two summers in the 1950s. One can only hope for a revival.

Fort Knox is on Route 174 just west of Route 1 at the Penobscot River. Managed as a state historic park, it is open daily 9:00 A.M. to sunset. Admission is $1.50. A flashlight is helpful for exploring some of the long, dark, and eerie chambers.

Off the Beaten Path
Down East

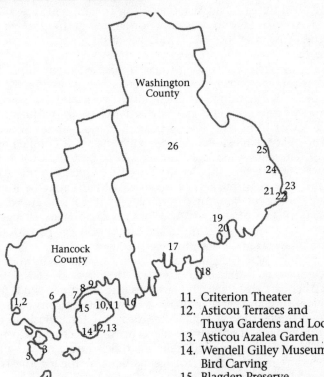

Washington
County

26

25

24

21 23
22

19
20

17

Hancock
County

18

8 9
6 7
1,2   15 10,11 16
14 12,13

5 3

4

11. Criterion Theater
12. Asticou Terraces and
    Thuya Gardens and Lodge
13. Asticou Azalea Garden
14. Wendell Gilley Museum of
    Bird Carving
15. Blagden Preserve
16. Schoodic Point
17. Ruggles House
18. Great Wass Island
19. Burnham Tavern
20. Gates House
21. Old Sardine Village Museum
22. West Quoddy Head
23. Roosevelt Campobello
    International Park and
    Natural Area
24. Reversing Falls Park
25. St. Croix Island
26. Airline Road

1. Wilson Museum
2. *State of Maine*
3. Haystack Mountain School
   of Crafts
4. Isle au Haut
5. Crockett Cove Woods
   Preserve
6. Parson Fisher House
7. Colonel Black Mansion
8. Stanwood Homestead and
   Birdsacre Sanctuary
9. Lamoine State Park
10. Natural History Museum

DOWN EAST

Where "down east" Maine begins is a matter of some debate and conjecture. The term dates back to early sailing days, when vessels heading east had the prevailing coastal winds at their stern, making an easy go of it from Portland to Eastport. Heading back the other way into the winds was a different matter altogether.

Eighteen-wheelers have long since supplanted cargo ships, but the term lingers. Today, down east refers almost as much to a notion as a destination. The classic down east landscape ranges from rocky promontories ceaselessly battered by surf to quiet harborside towns filled with lobster boats in various states of disrepair. The image of down east Maine may vary, but it's unified by a sense of remoteness and isolation, as well as by the idea that it's populated by a laconic, hard-bitten breed that seems to thrive on adversity. Although pockets of down east Maine may be found west of Penobscot Bay, for the most part it doesn't appear in earnest until east of the bay. And for real aficionados of rugged Maine, down east doesn't quite start until you get past Mount Desert and average tides start to exceed 20 feet.

No matter where that imaginary down east line is drawn, east of Bucksport you'll start finding yourself in classic coastal Maine. The farther east you head, the fewer tourist amenities you'll find and the grittier and more ineffably authentic the towns become. And then there's the fog, which seems to cling tenaciously to the coast through much of the year. If you arrive expecting fog you're less likely to be disappointed. Take the time to note how the fog enhances the richness of the foliage, particularly the fog forests in the Deer Isle area and the heaths near Cutler.

HANCOCK COUNTY

Hancock County contains Maine's crown jewels: Mount Desert and Acadia National Park. But don't be blinded by this dazzling display. Be sure to explore the rest of the county, particularly Deer Isle, which doesn't attract nearly such numbers as its more famous island cousin to the east. The county also extends far inland to the northeast, where you'll find remote lakes, good fishing, and unpretentious small towns.

Castine Area

If you've ever wondered what America looked like before Dutch elm disease, head to the quiet coastal town of Castine, about 16 miles south of Route 1. This regal village, where the occasional house that's *not* of white clapboard stands out like a drunkard at a debutante ball, is overarched throughout by towering, majestic elms. Look closely and you'll see small numbered tags on the trees, indications of the town's tireless efforts to keep the canopy healthy and alive. When signs of disease appear, arborists rush in like a SWAT team. Castine's success rate is admirable, and it's hard not to get a little nostalgic about all the long-gone elms that once graced cities and small towns across the country.

The elms are only part of Castine's allure. There's also the rich and sometimes bizarre military history. In the seventeenth and eighteenth centuries, the town passed back and forth between the French and British at a dizzying rate. Among the luminaries who made appearances in Castine was Miles Standish, who in 1635 was dispatched to aid the British colonists in their resistance against French usurpers. The small band accompanying Standish was unsuccessful, and the French maintained control except for a brief interregnum when newly aggressive Dutch prevailed. Around 1700 the British once again reclaimed the town and held it, more or less, until the Revolution.

During the Revolutionary War, one of the more ignominious American defeats took place when forty-four American ships failed to defeat the thinly defended British fort. A British fleet then forced the Americans to retreat upriver, where the colonists scuttled all ships to avoid capture and returned to Boston on foot. Among those court-martialed for their cowardice in this episode was Paul Revere, the famed silversmith and sentinel; his military career never quite recovered from this ignoble setback. You can learn about these historic episodes at a number of markers throughout the town, as well as at the earthworks marking the sites of Fort George and Fort Madison. On your way into town, look for the remains of the British canal between Hatch's and Wadsworth coves, which was constructed during the War of 1812 (when the British *again* occupied Castine).

The best way to enjoy Castine is to take a walking tour of the quiet, shady streets. Ask for one of the well-written and highly informative walking tour brochures produced by the Castine Merchants' Association, available free at many shops and restaurants.

In addition to the walking tour, several sites lend themselves to brief visits, including Dyce's Head Light at the westernmost point of town; follow Battle Avenue to the western end. Although this 1828 lighthouse is closed to the public (it was replaced by an offshore navigational beacon in the 1930s), there are a couple of trails that lead below the lighthouse to rocky bluffs overlooking Penobscot Bay, perfect for an afternoon picnic or an evening sunset walk. Look for the small sign near the lighthouse indicating PUBLIC TRAIL.

On Perkins Street stop by the **Wilson Museum** and the adjacent Perkins House. This small brick museum overlooking the water was built in 1921 to house the anthropological collections of local resident John Howard Wilson. Represented are a broad array of crafts and tools from native cultures worldwide, including cultures of Peru, Ethiopia, Angola, Oceania, and Venezuela. Spears and other weapons from Java and the Philippines fill another case, and the museum houses a display of rifles dating from 1580 to the 1880s. American history buffs will enjoy the replica of the 1805 American kitchen downstairs, as well as the operating blacksmith forge next door. And don't miss the outbuilding featuring the display of winter and summer hearses.

At the John Perkins House next door you can tour the oldest home in Castine. Miraculously (or perhaps not so miraculously), the house emerged intact despite British bombardment during the wars. This trim colonial house was also appropriated for British officers' quarters during both the Revolution and War of 1812. Guided tours of the house in the summer include demonstrations of open-hearth cooking, with guests invited to taste the results.

The museum and the house are open from the end of May to the end of September daily except Monday 2:00 to 5:00 P.M. (The blacksmith shop is open Wednesdays and Sundays in July and August.) Museum admission is free; Perkins House tours are $2.

Castine is an almost perfectly preserved village, but there's one towering anachronism: The *State of Maine,* a hulking gray former troop ship berthed at the docks of the Maine Maritime Academy, one of five academies nationwide training merchant marines. The ship, which rises incongruously over the village, was built in 1952 as the USS *Upshur;* after it was decommissioned, it was provided to the academy as a training vessel. Cadets spend sixty days at sea during the course of their training, either as "deckies" or as engineers. The ship can house up to five hundred cadets and staff. Its interior has the familiar feel of a large urban high school, with extensive linoleum and traditional off-hue paint slathered thickly on the walls (although notably lacking in graffiti). Midshipmen give guided tours of the ship in July and August, when the academy is not in session. Tours last about forty-five minutes and are free of charge. Call for a tour schedule: 326–4311.

Deer Isle

The drive from Castine to Stonington takes you through rolling countryside with glimpses of Penobscot Bay and beyond. (A driving detour through Cape Rosier peninsula, a pastoral cul-de-sac of early homes and rich landscapes, is an appealing if somewhat indirect route south.) Near Sargentville you'll cross a high, narrow suspension bridge across Eggemoggin Reach to Deer Isle. The bridge was built in 1938, but Deer Isle still retains a subdued and islandlike feel in its villages and rural byways. Like so many coastal Maine communities, the villages of Deer Isle look to the sea. The bridge offers access through the back door.

A scenic drive from the village of Deer Isle will take you along Stinson Neck to the nationally known **Haystack Mountain School of Crafts,** certainly one of the most scenic campuses anywhere in the nation. This summer crafts school offers instruction to about eighty students per session. Its campus was designed in the early 1960s by architect Edward Larrabee Barnes, who was faced with a rugged site consisting of a steep, spruce-studded hillside plunging into the waters of Jericho Bay. Instead of building at the top or bottom of the slope, as many presumed he would, Barnes daringly designed a campus hugging the slope, with dramatic water views from virtually every building and walkway. And instead of disrupting the delicate spruce, moss, and granite hillside with intrusive construction, he designed twenty small shingled buildings that were placed on footings above the ground and connected by "floating" wooden staircases and boardwalks. A broad central stairway serves as a main hallway, descending to the Flag Deck with its spectacular vistas of gently domed offshore islands capped with the sharp tips of spruce trees.

Visitors are welcome to walk to the Flag Deck and visit the college store, "Goods in the Woods," which sells art supplies and craft books. During the instructional sessions the smells of the ocean and the spruce mingle with the sounds of reggae and wood saws. A nature trail near the shop is also open to the public, but the studios may not be visited except by prior arrangement. Campus tours are offered daily at 1:00 P.M. between June 1 and August 31. Incidentally, don't look for Haystack Mountain hereabouts. The school was named after a mountain near the campus's former location.

To reach the Haystack Mountain School of Crafts on Stinson Neck, drive south of the village of Deer Isle on Route 15 to the second Gulf station, then turn left (there's a small sign) and follow this road for 7 miles. The campus driveway is well marked. For more information call 348–2306.

Continuing southward on Route 15, you'll soon arrive at village of Stonington. This southernmost point of Deer Isle can seem remote and desolate, particularly when the fog rolls in and the low, lugubrious moan of the foghorn reverberates along the coast. When the weather is clear, pocket-sized islands clutter the horizon and in the distance the gentle peaks of Isle au Haut rise steely blue above the scene. Stonington is a true fisherman's village. Except for a few crafts and antiques dealers, it retains a salty, gritty feel. You'll be disappointed if you're looking for fancy inns and restaurants; Stonington offers basic food and accommodations in its several restaurants, motels, and bed and breakfasts.

To really get a feel for the area, plan to abandon your car for a while. Two good alternatives are available: You can travel by sea kayak for anywhere between a few hours and a week among the dozens of islands off Stonington. Or you can venture by mail boat to Isle au Haut to explore on foot Acadia National Park's most remote and wild section.

Sea kayaking has caught on in Maine over the past decade, and anywhere along the coast you're likely to see the graceful, slender craft making their way across open waters to once-remote islands. The sport has been compared to mountain biking on water, and that's an apt analogy. Among Maine sea kayakers the Stonington area is perhaps the most popular. Of the many small islands in the area, a good number are publicly owned and allow camping. The Nature Conservancy also owns several of the islands (day use only), one of which is used to pasture a large flock of sheep.

Along Merchant's Row—the local name for the archipelago off Stonington—the islands are rimmed with weathered pink granite that becomes infused with an almost phosphorescent glow at sunset. Exploring one of these miniature wildernesses is an experience like no other in Maine.

With unpredictable wind and fog, the coast's weather conditions are highly volatile. It's best to have some oceangoing experience before renting a kayak and setting out on your own. Failing that, another option is to sign up for a trip with Explorers at Sea, an outfitter based on the Stonington waterfront. They provide all the equipment you'll need, along with meals, a guide, and enough instruction to get you where you're going. No experience is necessary, but you'll enjoy yourself more if you're reasonably fit and comfortable on the water. Gliding across the bay, you'll likely discover that there's something very human and peaceable about the pace and scale of kayaking across open waters.

Explorers at Sea is located on Main Street in Stonington. Trips range from half-day harbor excursions ($50) to five-day expeditions ($575). For more information call 367–2356.

If your outdoor tastes run more to hiking, plan to board one of the mail boats to **Isle au Haut,** so named in 1604 by French navigator Samuel de Champlain. (It means simply "high island.") About half of this big, brawny island is privately owned; the other half, about 2,800 acres, was donated to Acadia National Park. Depending on which boat you take from Stonington, you'll be deposited either at the village of Isle au Haut or, farther along, at remote and hidden Duck Harbor.

The most dramatic trails leave from near the dock at Duck Harbor, where five Adirondack-style lean-tos are maintained for campers. (Camping reservations are essential. Call Acadia National Park at 288–3338.) After disembarking, follow Western Head Road—a grassy, wooded lane—to Western Head Trail. This connects to Cliff and Goat trails, which wind their way between spectacular, rocky shoreline and damp, dense forests of fir, spruce, moss, and lichens. From the Goat Trail you can climb to the bald summit of Duck Harbor Mountain, which provides surprisingly open views of the island and eastern Penobscot Bay, including the eastern shore of Vinalhaven Island. From here you can return to the harbor in plenty of time for the return boat. Be sure to pack a picnic lunch to enjoy along one of the many cobblestone beaches, since no food is available in the park. A water pump for drinking water is located at Duck Harbor; fill up your canteens before you set off.

If you're curious about island culture, you can disembark at the village, visit the general store and the Union Congregational Church, then walk on trails or along a dirt road 4 miles to Duck Harbor for the return trip. (That itinerary may easily be reversed.) Visitors usually have about six hours to explore the island. A ranger meets incoming boats to provide maps and hiking information.

Round trip fare is $17 for adults; $8 for children under twelve. Isle au Haut Ferry Service does not take reservations, but they turn away surprisingly few passengers from their twice-daily boats. Plan to arrive at the Atlantic Avenue Hardware Dock in Stonington thirty minutes before departure. For a current schedule call 367–5193.

Before you depart Deer Isle, take time to visit the Nature Conservancy's **Crockett Cove Woods Preserve,** located a few minutes northwest of Stonington. This one-hundred-acre preserve contains a fog forest: a rich, quiet, mossy forest of mature spruce, fir, and pine that thrives in the damp, foggy environment prevalent along Deer Isle's south coast. Walking along the short self-guided nature path, you'll hear bird songs filter through the forest and enjoy the contrast of the rough bark of the red spruce against the brilliant green of the soft mosses. Brochures describing some of the natural highlights may be found in the registration box near the entrance. The preserve is open during daylight hours, and no admission is charged. From Stonington, head northwest on the road toward the town of Sunset. Shortly after passing through the village of Burnt Cove, turn left on Whitman Road. Follow along the cove until the pavement ends and a dirt road departs to the right. Drive 150 yards to a small parking area with a registration box.

Blue Hill and Environs

Heading farther down east, you'll soon pass through the coastal town of Blue Hill, named after the gently rounded 934-foot hill that dominates the relatively low terrain hereabouts. This aristocratic town, located at the head of Blue Hill Harbor, boasts dozens of historically significant buildings dating from the last century and earlier. For the last two decades or so, Blue Hill has also served as a magnet for a variety of potters, weavers, and other craftspeople, many of whom sell their wares in shops in the village and outlying areas. Blue Hill is also home to many fine inns and restaurants, and for many decades it has been a popular summer destination for those looking for a somewhat less social season than on Mount Desert Island.

If there's any one historical character who defines Blue Hill, it's Parson Jonathan Fisher, a Harvard-educated cleric who became the village's first settled minister in 1796. Parson Fisher, who lived in Blue Hill for more than half a century, is considered a New England original of the highest order: he was a respected painter, writer, minister, and tinkerer whose energies were indefatigable. His *Morning View of Blue Hill Village* is an enduring primitive American landscape (the painting can be viewed at the Farnsworth Museum in Rockland), and the journal he kept faithfully for fifty-nine years remains a source of interest to scholars and historians.

The **Parson Fisher House,** built in 1814, is open to the public as a memorial to Fisher's many talents. The two-story, four-room house, which Fisher himself built, contains his elegant home-made furniture, copies of books he bound himself, prints and originals of Fisher paintings, maps he surveyed, and examples of the style of shorthand he invented. Of particular interest is a clock with wooden works Fisher made while at Harvard; its painted face represents the five languages he spoke (and used in delivering sermons)—Hebrew, Latin, French, Greek, and Aramaic. About the only thing Fisher wasn't interested in, according to historians, was politics.

The Parson Fisher House is about a half mile south of Blue Hill village on Routes 15 and 176. It is open from the end of May until early September, daily except Sunday, 2:00 to 5:00 P.M. Admission is $2. For more information call 374–2459.

Also in Blue Hill is the foursquare Holt House, home of the Blue Hill Historical Society. Located at the head of the harbor, the home was built in 1815 by one of the first families to settle in Blue Hill. The home was purchased by the Blue Hill Historical Society in 1970 and restored to its earlier appearance. Some of the original stenciling was found beneath the wallpaper and reproduced throughout the home. The collection of local historic artifacts includes furniture, clocks, and kitchenware and continues to grow through donations and purchases. Holt House is open in July and August Tuesdays and Fridays 1:00 to 4:00 P.M.

If the weather's cooperative, you might consider a hike up eponymous Blue Hill for a superb view across Blue Hill Bay to the mountains of Mount Desert Island. Drive north on Route 172 and turn left (westward) on the road across from the Blue Hill Fairgrounds. Drive 0.8 mile to the sign marking the start of the trail on the right side of the road. The mile-long hike to the bald, craggy summit (topped with an unmanned fire tower) takes about forty-five minutes.

Ellsworth Area

In the mind of many, the town of Ellsworth is just a gateway to Mount Desert Island and Acadia National Park. This is a shame, since the town has a couple of sites that are well worth visiting. The **Colonel Black Mansion,** located just west of town center, is a fine example of a modified Georgian brick residence. Colonel John Black was a land agent for William Bingham, owner of two million acres of Maine; Black constructed this house between 1824 and 1827. Tradition says that the bricks were shipped from Philadelphia and the laborers from Boston. Of note are the triple-hung front windows (note the absence of a front door on the porch—residents entered and departed through the fully opened windows) and the handsome spiral staircase inside. Although the mansion was a full-time residence and office for the colonel, the house was used sparingly by his descendants. In 1930 the home, fully furnished right down to the original family linens, was donated to the county by Black's grandson.

The mansion, set amid 150 wooded acres, is a treasure trove of life in the nineteenth century. The house contains a canopied bed with the original tassels, a rare Aaron Willard clock, and an exceptional collection of blue and white pottery. There are a number of other Victorian flourishes, such as the stuffed peacock (which once roamed the grounds) and German silver bathing tub.

The mansion is open June 1 to October 15 every day except Sunday, 10:00 A.M. to 5:00 P.M. Forty-five-minute tours are held on the hour and half hour and cost $4 for adults and $2 for children under twelve. Located on Route 172 one-quarter mile south of Route 1. Call 667–8671.

On Route 3 about a mile south of Ellsworth (en route to Mount Desert) you'll pass on the right **Stanwood Homestead** and **Birdsacre Sanctuary.** The home was built in 1850 by Captain Leland Stanwood, the father of one of the country's most talented self-trained ornithologists. Cordelia Johnson Stanwood (1865–1958) contributed greatly to the understanding of the natural history and migration patterns of many North American birds, often using the woods behind her simple Cape-style home as an outdoor laboratory.

Today the house and grounds are owned and operated by the Stanwood Wildlife Foundation. The home, with its wide, worn pine board floors, houses many stuffed birds and an exceptional egg collection, along with period furniture and old photographs. The 130-acre grounds are laced with well-marked nature trails that wind past small ponds and through shady glades. The sanctuary is just yards off the busy highway but has a settled and quiet air. Cages behind the house are used for the rehabilitation of injured birds brought to the sanctuary and may house great horned owls, geese, and red-tailed hawks. There's even a "night deposit" for injured birds found after hours.

Admission to the sanctuary is free. Tours of the homestead (open daily 10:00 A.M. to 4:00 P.M.) are $2.50 for adults and 50 cents for children. Look closely for the entrance on Route 3; it's on the west side across from the Prompto 10-Minute Oil Change. For more information, call 667–8460.

Mount Desert Island

Acadia National Park on Mount Desert Island is the second most popular national park in the United States, eclipsed only by the Great Smoky Mountains. In 1990 more than five million park visits were recorded, with the number rising steadily. Between July 4 and Labor Day weekend, the island can literally fill up, leaving no place to pitch a tent or rent a room. Reservations are strongly encouraged during the peak season.

Getting off the beaten path at Mount Desert (pronounced de-SERT) is a matter more of strategy than of destination. Many visitors display a singular lack of imagination by stopping at Bar Harbor for an hour or two, then hopping on the park loop road ($5 per vehicle; pass is good for one week) to drive from one parking lot to another, rarely walking more than a few dozen yards from the road. Admittedly, the coastal loop road *is* spectacular, with twists and turns and views across Frenchman's Bay. But a motor tour provides only a glimpse of the spirit of the place, like viewing the countryside from an interstate highway. Detouring off the loop road and exploring by foot or boat offers a more intimate look at this remarkable island.

Acadia National Park offers no backcountry camping and only two drive-in campgrounds, both of which often fill up by early morning in midsummer. (Credit card reservations are accepted at Blackwoods Campground up to eight weeks in advance for arrival after June 15; call 800–451–1111.) In addition to the numerous private campgrounds, there is another, little-known option for campers: **Lamoine State Park,** located on the mainland 11 miles from the Acadia visitor center. The fifty-five-acre park is located on Eastern Bay and has a number of pleasant private campsites, including several overlooking the water. There's a boat launch, a pier for fishing, grassy fields, and picnic tables looking across the bay toward Cadillac Mountain and other Acadia peaks. It's a peaceful and quiet place and makes a good spot to unwind after a day in the park. There's but one disadvantage: no showers. (Public showers may be found near Blackwoods Campground.) Park managers report that the campsites rarely sell out, even on holiday weekends.

Immediately after crossing the Mount Desert Island causeway on Route 3, stop at the park visitor center at Hull's Cove to pick up a map. While there, ask for the park's hiking brochure, which lists some of the more than one hundred miles of trail in the park. The center is open 8:00 A.M. to 8:00 P.M. daily. For more information call 288–4932.

A good introduction to island ecology may be found at the **Natural History Museum** at the College of the Atlantic. This small liberal arts college, founded in 1969, prides itself on its strong environmental focus. The museum is housed in Turrets, a splendid stone mansion built in 1895 for John Josiah Emery. Two rooms on the first floor are filled with exhibits of animals typically found on Mount Desert, ranging from black bear (at least six are thought still to inhabit the west side of the island) to river otter. These fine displays of taxidermy are all prepared by college students, and more than fifty species are represented. On the front porch you'll find sweeping views across the harbor and the

Porcupine Islands—the view alone is worth the price of admission—as well as a small "touch tank" for children to experience local marine life.

The museum is on Route 3 just south of the Bluenose Ferry Terminal and is open mid-June to September 1, 9:00 A.M. to 5:00 P.M. daily. Admission is $2.50 for adults, $1.50 for seniors, 50 cents for children under twelve. Lectures are scheduled throughout the summer. Call for more information: 288–5015.

It's not hard to imagine Bar Harbor, the island's undisputed commercial center, during its belle epoch, when corporate titans and others maintained magnificent summer "cottages" (read: palaces) along the coastal hills. Think of Bar Harbor at the turn of the century as Newport, Rhode Island, with moosehorns. The Vanderbilts and the Rockefellers were among the families that established summer estates here; in fact, the national park's existence is due in large part to the generosity of these and other wealthy families, who purchased the more spectacular parts of the island and donated them to the U.S. government. (John D. Rockefeller Jr. alone donated 11,000 acres.) Although many fine homes may be viewed at a distance from here and there, the majority were destroyed during an extraordinary conflagration in the summer of 1947, a period of prolonged drought that bred wildfires throughout much of the state. Downtown Bar Harbor was spared, as were some of the year-round homes.

Much of Bar Harbor today caters to the tourist trade, and visitors can select from a wide array of T-shirt shops, restaurants, and bars. One site that retains some of the flavor of the town's heyday is the **Criterion Theater,** a magnificent 1932 theater that has retained its art deco extravagance. The interior of this 916-seat theater is awash with geometric patterns rendered in soft, earthy colors that seem enhanced in the dim glow of the central lamp. The theater, listed on the National Register of Historic Places, shows first-run films as well as classics. Splurge and pay extra for a seat in the loges, with boxlike seating and privacy partitions. The theater is located downtown on Cottage Street. For a recorded announcement of the current show, call 288–3441.

Some time around 1905 a rancorous local debate erupted over whether to allow automobiles onto the island or not. Progress, such as it was, eventually prevailed and horseless carriages were given run of the island, forever disrupting the tranquillity of the place. One of the outflanked opponents was John D. Rockefeller

Jr. Preferring to get even rather than get mad, he set about design-ing and building a 57-mile network of quiet, leafy carriage roads on the east side of the island, concentrated mostly around Jordan Pond. Rarely has vengeance produced so exquisite a result. The peaceful lanes blend remarkably well with the landscape and include a dozen graceful bridges crafted of local granite. The roads have suffered somewhat from age and neglect, but the spirit of the endeavor still shines through.

Carriages today are few, but mountain bikes are plentiful and, it turns out, are perfect vehicles for exploring "Mr. Rockefeller's roads." Pack a picnic lunch to enjoy along a stream, or take a side trip on foot for a summit view across the bay. You might also make a detour for outdoor tea and popovers at the Jordan Pond House, a longtime park landmark. The restaurant was opened in the 1870s but burned and was replaced in 1979. Tea is served between 2:30 and 5:30 P.M.; the restaurant is also open for lunch and dinner. Expect a wait for tea. Call 276–3316.

If you didn't bring a mountain bike, rentals are available in Bar Harbor at Acadia Bike Rentals (48 Cottage Street; 288–9605) and Bar Harbor Bicycle Shop (141 Cottage Street; 288–3886). In South-west Harbor try Southwest Cycle (Main Street; 244–5856). Bike shops can provide maps of the carriage roads, and their staff can make suggestions for day trips.

If you're in a horticultural frame of mind, head southward on Route 3 toward Northeast Harbor, where you can visit a pair of extraordinary hidden gardens that are as seldom visited as they are spectacular. The best (but not only) access to the **Asticou Terraces and Thuya Gardens and Lodge** is from a discrete parking lot off Route 3. Look for a small sign reading Asticou Ter-races on the left as you wind around Northeast Harbor coming from Seal Harbor. If you pass the grand Asticou Inn, you've gone too far. The lot is one-half mile south of the intersection of Routes 198 and 3.

A paved trail leads down to the water and is worth a short stroll. But be sure to cross the highway and begin the climb up the granite steps and through a series of stone terraces overlook-ing the harbor. The landscaping is remarkable: It seems rugged and wild and ineffably Maine, but is actually one of the finer bits of outdoor architecture in the state. The hillside was created by Boston landscape architect Joseph Henry Curtis (1841–1928), who summered here for many years and donated the land and his lodge as a "gift for the quiet recreation of the people of this town and their summer guests." At the top of the hill, Curtis's rustic Thuya Lodge (named after the scientific name for white cedar, *Thuya occidentalis*) is open to the public and contains an assortment of antiques and a fine horticultural library.

Behind the lodge, walk through the massive carved wooden gates into the formal Thuya Gardens, with reflecting pool, gazebo, spectacular flower displays, and lawns trimmed as precisely as putting greens. If the weather's nice, you're certain to find people reading here, talking quietly, or examining the wide variety of common and exotic flowers. The garden was designed by Charles K. Savage, who borrowed elements from famed English designer Gertrude Jekyll and Maine landscape designer Beatrix Farrand.

The terraces and garden are open July 1 to Labor Day 7:00 A.M. to 7:00 P.M. daily. The lodge is open daily 10:00 A.M. to 4:30 P.M. A $2 donation is requested of visitors to the gardens. The lodge and garden is also accessible by car without ascending the terraces. Head toward Seal Cove from the terraces' parking lot for about one-fifth mile and turn left on the first road. This will bring you to the lodge. For more information call 276–5130.

Just north of the Asticou Inn is the **Asticou Azalea Garden.** These grounds, like the Thuya Gardens, were also designed by Charles Savage but have a vastly different structure and feel. Raked gravel walkways wind through the flower beds, with elements borrowed from both East and West. Benches are tucked into leafy niches here and there, providing for a quiet moment or two. A sand garden, designed after those found in Kyoto, Japan, in the late fifteenth century, invites a pause. The gardens are small—only two and a half acres—but in their design they recall a spacious home, with one private room opening into another. Although lush and inviting throughout the summer, the gardens are at their most spectacular during the last three weeks in June, when many of the fifty varieties of azalea are in bloom.

The garden is located about 100 yards north of the intersection of Routes 3 and 198; look for a parking lot on the east side of the road. Open during daylight hours April 1 to October 31. Admission is free.

From picturesque and snug Northeast Harbor, boats depart regularly for the Cranberry Islands, a pleasant archipelago of flat, open islands dotted with summer homes and cranberry bogs. Several options are available to prospective visitors. You can travel with a National Park Service naturalist to outermost Baker Island and spend a couple of hours exploring the delicate, dramatic terrain; or take the scheduled ferry to either Great or Little Cranberry Islands and explore on your own. Neither island boasts much in the way of tourist attractions, and most residents would like to keep it that way. Great Cranberry has a gift shop, grocery store, and small lunch spot open Thursdays through Mondays. Isleford, on Little Cranberry, has about the same with the addition of the Isleford Historical Museum, a small collection focusing on island history and maintained by the National Park Service. Open daily 9:45 A.M. to 4:30 P.M.; admission is free.

Beal and Bunker (244–3575) offers six boats daily to the Cranberry Islands. Round trip cost is $6 for adults and $3 for children under twelve. Isleford Ferry Company (276–3717) offers a daily two-hour nature cruise, including a brief stop at Isleford, $7 for adults and $5 for children under twelve. A daily four-and-a-half-hour naturalist cruise to Baker Island costs $12 adults and $7 children.

In 1930 a Southwest Harbor plumber named Wendell Gilley set off to study a display of taxidermy at the Boston Museum of Natural History. What caught this amateur taxidermist's attention, however, was a display of delicately carved wooden birds. Gilley returned to Maine to take up a new hobby. By the time of his death fifty years later, Gilley was established as one of the nation's foremost carvers of birds. Carvings by Gilley and other master carvers may be seen at the **Wendell Gilley Museum of Bird Carving** just north of the town of Southwest Harbor on Route 102.

This modern and airy museum, built in 1981, contains about 250 carvings, ranging from miniature songbirds such as chickadees and mourning doves to massive life-sized eagles and turkeys. After looking at some of Gilley's fine handiwork, you can watch a half-hour video about Gilley and his woodcarving, then watch a woodcarver-in-residence at work in the glass-walled studio. One- and four-day wood-carving classes are offered throughout the summer (tuition includes "printed materials, wood, paints, Band-Aids and other supplies"). A small gift shop sells carved birds ranging in price from $50 to $500.

The Wendell Gilley Museum is open May through December. July and August hours are 10:00 A.M. to 5:00 P.M. daily except

Monday. June, September, and October, 10:00 A.M. to 4:00 P.M. daily except Monday. May, November, and December, Friday through Sunday 10:00 A.M. to 4:00 P.M. Admission is $3 for adults and $1 for children under twelve. For more information call 244–7555.

The west side of Mount Desert is less populated and more forested than the dramatic, congested east side. Acadia National Park maintains a handful of hiking trails here, and gentle, winding roads touch the water at several points. Connoisseurs of country drives will enjoy exploring the roads around Bass Harbor and Seal Cove.

On the northwest side of the island, stop at Indian Point, site of the Nature Conservancy's **Blagden Preserve.** This 110-acre preserve features about 1,000 feet of shore frontage and a series of meandering, attractive walking trails through mixed hardwood and softwood forest. Bring binoculars and a book to the rocky shore, where the caretakers have scattered a dozen or so red Adirondack-style chairs facing westward across the water toward Blue Hill. Keep an eye out for harbor seals, which commonly haul themselves out to rest on the rocky ledges offshore on sunny days. In the forest near the shores you might also spot (as I did one day) a pileated woodpecker or an osprey. Although the preserve officially closes at 6:00 P.M., the caretakers often allow visitors to enjoy the sunsets over Blue Hill Bay before closing the gate.

The preserve is located off Indian Point Road. From the park visitor center at Hulls Cove, head south on Route 198 toward Somesville. Shortly after passing the Spruce Valley Campground, turn right on Indian Point Road. Proceed 1.7 miles to a fork; bear right for another 200 yards. Look for preserve entrance on right amid a row of handsome oaks. Stop at the red caretaker's cottage to sign in and obtain a preserve map.

One of the less-visited parts of Acadia National Park accessible by car is located a 45-mile drive eastward from Mount Desert. But **Schoodic Point,** an isolated, rugged promontory, is well worth the drive. From the town of Winter Harbor, follow the National Park Service sign for Schoodic Peninsula. A winding one-way road soon takes you along the east side of Frenchman Bay; on a clear day, magnificent views of Cadillac Mountain open up through the spruce and pine. At the tip a broad expanse of salmon-pink granite angles down to the water's edge, and the ocean tends to be at its most restless here. Bring a picnic; no food is available south of Winter Harbor. Another one-way road leads back along the other side of the spruce-clad peninsula toward the town of Corea. Take it slow and stop at the waysides to enjoy the unfolding show.

WASHINGTON COUNTY

East of Schoodic Point the coast's character begins to change. Shops and restaurants cater to locals rather than travelers. In the harbors lobster boats far outnumber the yachts. Homes are maintained less to impress visitors than to provide sanctuary during the long months of winter. Coastal villages become somewhat more rough-hewn, reflecting a changing ratio of fishermen over summer folk. Down east Maine begins here in earnest.

Heading eastward on Route 1, you'll pass through the towns of Steuben, Milbridge, Cherryfield, and Harrington. Take time to enjoy the architecture along the way, particularly in Milbridge and Cherryfield, where many of the mansions reflect the boom days of the lumber, shipbuilding, and fishing trades. (A good number of the finer Milbridge homes have been converted to B&Bs.)

Jonesport and Vicinity

In Columbia Falls the **Ruggles House** is open to the public and offers a clear look into the region's past. This graceful but modest early nineteenth-century home was constructed for Thomas Ruggles, who moved to town in 1790 aiming to make his fortune in lumber. Ruggles succeeded in his quest and soon became a respected community leader, eventually appointed to a judgeship in Machias. In 1818 he commissioned a twenty-two-year-old architect, Aaron S. Sherman, to design his home.

The interior has several elements of architectural distinction, including a magnificent flying staircase in the central hallway, "open Bible" keystones above the Palladian arches, and pine doors hand painted to resemble mahogany. Of particular note is the intricate wood carving throughout the parlor; local lore asserts the carving was executed by a British craftsman who labored three years with a penknife. The home, which was restored from a state of severe dilapidation in 1950, now contains much of Ruggles's original furniture.

The Ruggles House is open June to mid-October, Monday to Saturday 9:30 A.M. to 4:30 P.M. and Sundays 11:00 A.M. to 4:30 P.M. Tours run about twenty minutes. Donations are encouraged. The house is one-quarter mile off Route 1 in the village of Columbia Falls.

One of the Nature Conservancy's most spectacular Maine holdings is on **Great Wass Island,** located south of Jonesport and accessible by car via bridge and causeway. This 1,579-acre preserve, acquired in 1978, has more than five hundred acres of jack pine—stunted, gnarly trees well suited to the harsh conditions on the island—as well as considerable areas of open heath and bog.

Two trails provide access to the eastern shore from a small parking lot. The trails, which twist over rocky and root-covered ground across relatively flat terrain, may be linked together by a hike along the rocky shoreline, making a loop about 5 miles long. Take some time along the ocean's edge to enjoy the views of the lighthouse on Mistake Island (also a Nature Conservancy holding) and to watch the seals congregating densely on the ledges offshore. Allow about three hours for the entire loop, and be prepared for damp conditions; fog often moves in with little warning.

The preserve parking lot is on the west side of Great Wass Island. From Jonesport cross the bridge to Beals Island and continue onward, bearing right at the fork after you cross the causeway to Great Wass. The pavement soon ends; continue until you pass a lobster pound at Black Duck Cove, then look for the lot on the left side of the road. Maps and a birder's checklist may be obtained at the registration box.

Machias Area

Here's a bit of Revolutionary War lore long buried in the footnotes: The first naval battle of the Revolution took place near the port town of Machias, when ambitious colonists succeeded in capturing the better-equipped British schooner *Margaretta.* The episode unfolded in June 1775, a month after the Battle of Lexington. The *Margaretta* arrived in Machias accompanying a freight ship to procure wood for British barracks in Boston. This didn't sit well with the citizenry of Machias, who hastily organized an expedition against the British ship. With two smaller ships they successfully attacked the *Margaretta,* mortally wounding the captain and capturing the crew. The story didn't have an entirely happy ending for the colonists. The British vowed retribution, and in subsequent months returned to rout Machias soldiers and burn many buildings.

One place to learn a bit about the battle for the *Margaretta* is **Burnnam Tavern,** a pale yellow gambrel-roofed building located on a small rise in the pleasant commercial town of Machias. Constructed in 1770 by Job Burnnam, the tavern served as the base from which Jeremiah O'Brien and his townsmen formulated plans for the attack on the British schooner. Following the skirmish, it was in the tavern that *Margaretta's* Captain More succumbed to his wounds and other British soldiers were nursed back to health.

The tavern was acquired and restored by the Daughters of the American Revolution in 1910 and today appears much as it did during the heady days of the War of Independence. The original tap table is on display, as are a tea set and a chest taken from the captured ship. Up the steep "good morning" stairs are several bedrooms, including one where local Masons first met in 1778. Today the rooms house a collection of tools and other historic objects.

The tavern is open mid-June to Labor Day, Monday through Friday 9:00 A.M. until 5:00 P.M. It is in the center of town just north of the Machias River on Route 192. Tours last about a half hour and cost $2 for adults and 25 cents for children. For more information call 255–4432.

A wooden model of the *Margaretta* may be seen at the **Gates House** in the riverside village of Machiasport, several miles south of Machias on Route 92. Built around 1807, this home was in the Gates family for more than a century before it became the headquarters of the Machiasport Historical Society. Located on the tidal river, this classic clapboarded home contains displays related to the marine history of the area and its early life and commerce. A kitchen displays early utensils; local period fashion may be seen upstairs. There's also a telescope offering views down the river toward the open ocean, allowing visitors to duplicate an act that must have been performed dozens of times daily when Machiasport was an active seaside town. The house is open June through mid-September Monday through Friday 12:30 to 4:30 P.M. Donations are encouraged. For more information call 255–8461.

If you're continuing eastward toward Lubec, consider the somewhat longer but more scenic trip via Route 191 through the harbor town of Cutler. Other than a U.S. Navy communications facility (with a massive ring of 900-foot antennae visible for many miles), there are no major landmarks along the route. But the road offers a fine view of coastal Maine at its most remote and least developed. Views of the ocean open here and there, and the road traverses broad heaths and blueberry barrens, which blaze a fiery red in fall.

Lubec Region

Maine's easternmost towns, located along Cobscook and Passamaquoddy bays, are known for two major distinctions: the booming sardine industry that flourished here at the turn of the century, and the mighty tides that sweep twice daily in and out of the bays. The difference between high tide and low can be as much as 28 feet near Lubec and Eastport, and each tide generates fiercely powerful currents that can stymie unwary boat captains attempting to make headway at the wrong time and the wrong place.

Some sardine canning operations still operate along the Maine coast, but the industry is just a shadow of its former self, when up to 120 million tins of Maine sardines were produced annually. The **Old Sardine Village Museum** in Lubec offers a look at that bygone era. Owned and operated by Barney and Becky Rier, who themselves owned and operated a sardine plant until 1960, this low, long barn with brick and concrete flooring contains a fascinating slice from the history of American commerce. While we take canned foods for granted now, they weren't always met with universal acceptance. Commercially canned foods grew in popularity around the Civil War, making fortunes for entrepreneurs and changing the way people thought about foods and seasons. Maine was one of the pioneers in the canning industry, and the Riers offer a rather comprehensive overview of the canning process. Among the more intriguing exhibits is one on "pearl essence." This paste obtained from herring skin during processing was often used to give nail polish a metallic sheen.

The museum is on Route 189 just west of Lubec and is open from mid-June to mid-September Wednesday through Sunday 1:00 to 5:00 P.M. Admission is $3 for adults; children are free with parents. For information call 733–2822.

Not far from the sardine museum is the easternmost point in the United States: **West Quoddy Head.** (East Quoddy Head, if you're wondering, is across the channel in Canada.) This narrow lobe of land extends off the mainland south of Lubec and is anchored by a distinctive candy-striped red and white lighthouse, one that's appeared on postage stamps and countless wall calendars. On an infrequent clear day, you can see to the cliffs of Grand Manan, a brawny Canadian island 16 miles out in the Bay of Fundy. The lighthouse, first commissioned in 1807 and rebuilt in 1858, is operated by the Coast Guard and closed to the public. But visitors may explore the grounds, which are often blooming with daylilies and wild roses. A short shoreline trail runs southward along a jagged, 50-foot precipice to Quoddy Head State Park, a 481-acre oceanside park with picnicking and limited hiking. During high and low tides you can witness the remarkable force of the currents as they eddy and curl around the offshore ledges and rocks.

The lighthouse grounds are open daily 8:00 A.M. to 7:00 P.M.; the state park is open daily from May 30 to October 15, 9:00 A.M. to sunset. No charge for visiting either site.

Campobello Island is accessible by bridge across The Narrows from the town of Lubec. Although the island is in the Canadian province of New Brunswick (expect a cursory customs check both coming and going), the United States has a stake in one section of the island: the **Roosevelt Campobello International Park and Natural Area.** This 2,800-acre park, located about 2 miles from the bridge, is managed by a special international commission with representatives from the U.S Department of Interior and Canada's Department of External Affairs. It claims to be the only park of this kind in the world, a bit of justification for including a wonderful Canadian destination in a book about Maine.

The park is named after U.S. President Franklin Delano Roosevelt, who summered here most every year between 1883, when he was one year old, and 1921, the summer he was striken with polio. FDR's father, James Roosevelt, was first lured to the island's beauty and tranquillity when Campobello was being touted as an

Lighthouse, West Quoddy Head

exclusive resort for the wealthy. He purchased four acres and a partially built home, completing the residence over the next few years. In 1910 the family moved to a significantly larger eighteen-bedroom "cottage" nearby, which was originally built in 1897. The cottage is open to the public.

Get an overview of the island's history at the visitor center, where you can watch a short film about FDR's long relationship with the island. (He introduced golf to the island; locals approved, since they could graze their sheep on the greens.) The maroon-shingled Roosevelt cottage is a short walk behind the visitor center. A self-guided tour allows a leisurely wander through the spacious homestead, which seems an appealing mix of the simple and the grandiose. It's hard to imagine an eighteen-bedroom house feeling like a home, but it does. Helpful guides are on hand to answer any questions you might have. It's easy to picture the extended Roosevelt clan gathered in the massive kitchen on the east side of the house during one of the region's foggy mornings.

Nearby is the equally elegant Hubbard Cottage, built in 1891 and often open to the public. (If it's closed, it usually means a conference is being held there.) A visit to this classic shingle-style home at the edge of the bay seems a trip to a lost era. The magnificent view across the water through the oval window in the dining room alone makes a visit worthwhile. If you'd like to spend more time outdoors, be sure to obtain a map of the park grounds at the visitor center. The park maintains about 8 miles of walking trails through a wide variety of terrain, including a dramatic 2-mile oceanside hike from Raccoon Beach to Liberty Point.

The park is open from Memorial Day weekend until mid-October, 9:00 A.M. to 5:00 P.M. Eastern Time. (Don't forget you're in Atlantic Time, one hour later, after you cross the bridge.) Admission is free. For more information call 506–752–2922.

Eastport and Vicinity

Turning from the ocean and heading toward inland Washington County, you'll wind along beautiful and surprisingly remote Cobscook and Passamaquoddy bays. Cobscook Bay State Park is one of the state's finest parks, with many of the secluded campsites located along the water on three peninsulas. A picnic area is near a broad, grassy meadow with fine views down to the water. The park is just off Route 1 (look for the sign) between Whiting and Dennysville.

Another commendable spot for a picnic is **Reversing Falls Park,** an unassuming municipally operated park 6 miles from the town of Pembroke. This 140-acre park is located on Mahar Point, where Dennys and Whiting bays squeeze into Cobscook Bay between the point and Falls Island. Because of the extraordinary tides, water tends to back up here, creating a set of rapids heading one way at one tide and reversing at the next. There's a short walk through mixed forest to the rocky edge of the river; several picnic tables invite a relaxed perusal of this natural phenomenon. The day I visited about a dozen seals were playing and leaping in the building current. The best time to visit, I'm told, is about two hours before high tide.

Several small signs point you from Pembroke to the park. Turn east at the IOOF Hall, then travel 3.4 miles along Leighton Neck to a right turn. Follow this road, which becomes increasingly rough, to the end and park. There is no charge for visiting the park, which is open during daylight hours.

After a short side trip to the cul-de-sac town of Eastport, with its rugged brick buildings and decidedly oceangoing air (and a rather surprising number of small restaurants), continue northward on Route 1. Between Robbinston and Calais there's a small island about a half mile offshore in the St. Croix River whose appearance is far overshadowed by its historical significance. **St. Croix Island** (so named after two large bays north of the island that appear to form the arms of a cross) was the site of the first attempted permanent European settlement in North America north of Florida.

In 1604 a group of some eighty French colonists under the guidance of Sieur de Monts and his lieutenant, Samuel de Champlain, landed on the island with the intent of establishing a village and trading center. The colonists were so uncertain of what to expect that they brought their own timber for building homes. The island was reasonably secure from surprise attack but lacked a number of amenities, including a ready supply of drinking water. In addition, the island was swept by bitter north winds, prompting Champlain to note that there were "six months of winter in this country." The following summer the colonists abandoned St. Croix Island and resettled at Annapolis Royale in Nova Scotia.

Saint Croix Island is managed as a national monument, but public transportation to the island is unavailable. A riverside observation area with historical markers is located along Route 1 near the town of Red Beach.

Calais Area

From this eastern corner of Maine, Route 1 heads north to Aroostook County (see "The County"), the road's character changing dramatically. Once you leave the sea at your back, few early homes line the road and salt air is replaced by the smell of spruce and fir. Timber companies own and manage a great deal of this land, which is filled with vast lakes and wild lakeshores. The region is highly popular among fishermen, hunters, and canoeists. The village of Grand Lake Stream, with its selection of lodges and boat access to numerous remote lakes, has been a favored base among many outdoorspeople for decades. Among the lodges here are Weatherbys (796–5558) and Colonial Sportsmen's Lodge (795–2655). Both cater to serious fishermen, but the owners make others feel welcome as well.

If you decide not to head northward from Calais, the quickest way back to the Maine Turnpike and points south is along Route 9, commonly known as the **Airline Road** or simply "the Airline." This straight shot across eastern Maine has roots back to 1857, when Calais citizens established a dirt path to improve mail service from the state's commercial hub at Bangor. In time the route was improved to accommodate stagecoaches, which made the trip daily except Sundays. The eighteen-hour trip was often brutal on passengers, but it was a full day quicker than traveling by steamship. When the steamship companies attempted to curb competition by depicting the route as populated by wolves and bandits, stagecoach ridership surged as adventurers shelled out the fare to claim they had survived the trip. Despite the incongruously modern-sounding name, the Airline is in fact the old name for the route, presumably to distinguish it from the competing Shore Line steamship company.

Today neither wolves nor bandits present much of a problem for motorists, but Route 9 does provide a glimpse at an interesting cross section of Maine. The road passes through thick spruce forests and cut-over timberland, across blueberry barrens and open heath. East of the town of Aurora, watch for the road to ascend a glacial esker (a tall ridge of gravel formed by currents running through massive tunnels beneath a melting glacier). The land seems to drop off on either side of the road as if on a man-made embankment; glacial bogs may be seen north of the road from a small rest area. There are few services along the road (an occasional hotel or snack bar), but for the most part it's just fast driving. In fact the Airline seems to be Maine's answer to the Autobahn. Even when driving over the speed limit you're likely to be passed by others evidently in a far greater hurry.

Off the Beaten Path in the North Woods

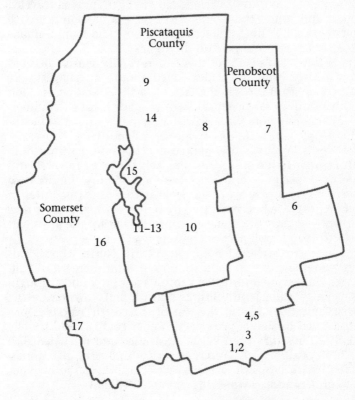

Piscataquis County

Penobscot County

9

14

8

7

Somerset County

15

6

11–13   10

16

4,5

3

1,2

17

1. Bangor Historical Society
2. Thomas Hill Standpipe
3. Hudson Museum
4. Indian Island
5. Old Town Canoe Company
6. Mattawamkeag Wilderness Park
7. Lumberman's Museum
8. Baxter State Park
9. North Maine Woods, Inc.
10. Katahdin Iron Works
11. SS *Katahdin*
12. Moosehead Marine Museum
13. Greenville Inn
14. Chesuncook Lake House
15. Mount Kineo
16. Moxie Falls
17. Floodproof Wire Bridge

NORTH WOODS

The North Woods consists of literally millions of acres of forest land, some of it as quiet and removed as when Thoreau traveled through and noted the "general stillness is more impressive than any sound." This is the terrain of moose and loon; humans don't so much linger as pass on through.

The North Woods isn't for the garden-variety tourist. Because the region is so wild and undeveloped, motor-car travelers may soon become frustrated at the lack of facilities and access. You can drive only so far on dusty logging roads through commercial timberland before you become a bit weary and start yearning for people and buildings of one sort or another.

The North Woods is best appreciated by those with outdoor inclinations: fishermen, hunters, white-water rafters, and canoeists. Especially canoeists. There are literally hundreds of miles of rivers and streams, as well as thousands of miles of lakeshore, that are best navigated by canoe. Footpaths exist here and there—notably the Appalachian Trail—but for the most part the North Woods trail network is sketchy at best.

One more brief caveat before you visit the North Woods: This is not wilderness. It's an industrial forest. And there's a big difference. Pockets of undisturbed forest may be found throughout—isolated state landholdings and property owned by the Nature Conservancy—but the rest of the North Woods is privately owned by about two dozen timber companies. Virtually the entire forest has been cut at least once and often twice. If you think of the North Woods as agricultural land, like a massive farm with crops on a forty-year rotation, you're on your way to understanding what this region is all about.

PENOBSCOT COUNTY

Penobscot County includes Maine's second city, the lumber capital of Bangor. But Bangor is a small urban oasis in country that ranges from rural to wild. The county's borders extend far to the north, striking deep into the heart of the timberlands north of the mill town of Millinocket.

Bangor Area

Maine's North Woods begins at the city of Bangor, both geographically and historically. Between 1820 and 1860, Bangor prospered like no other town in Maine as timber merchants employed hundreds of men to cut pine and spruce along the Penobscot and its tributaries, then float the logs down the river during great spring lumber drives. Once at the mills the logs were cut and exported throughout the nation and abroad. In fact Bangor was the largest lumber port in the world during the 1850s, and with that honor came tremendous prosperity. More than a few fortunes were made. Bangor began a decline in the 1880s as readily accessible trees were depleted; a fire destroyed much of the city in 1911. Nevertheless, Bangor retains much of historical interest, and it's not hard to imagine the place during its golden days more than a century ago.

A good place to get an overview of Bangor history is at the **Bangor Historical Society** at 159 Union Street (at the intersection of High Street). The collections are housed in an uncommonly graceful brick home constructed in 1836 for a prominent Bangor businessman. The first floor is furnished much like a typical Victorian home, with medallion-backed chairs, soaring gilded mirrors, and intricate Oriental carpets. Be sure to note the exceptional craftsmanship of the carved frieze and the Corinthian columns in the airy double parlor. Upstairs are galleries featuring exhibits related to Bangor's history. One-hour tours are offered Tuesday through Friday and on Sunday between noon and 4:00 P.M. For more information call 942–5766.

I can't precisely explain why, but the **Thomas Hill Standpipe,** built in 1898, is among my favorite architectural oddments in the state. Sited atop one of Bangor's gentle hills, the standpipe is essentially a water tank with an observation deck built around it. If nothing else, this 110-foot-high wooden structure attests to the pervasive influence of the shingle style in the late nineteenth century. With its clean lines, white shingles, and colonnaded overlook circling the top, the standpipe also provides a heartening glimpse into a world where even something as utilitarian as a water tank benefited from an architect's eye. The 1.75-million-gallon tank is still used today to provide water to the people of Bangor and is managed by the Bangor Water District. The standpipe

Thomas Hill Standpipe, Bangor

observatory may be appreciated from the outside anytime but is open to the public only once a year, usually during the first week in October, for fall foliage viewing. Call the Bangor Historical Society (942–5766) for the exact date.

All this history aside, Bangor today may be best known elsewhere in the nation as the home of "America's best-loved boogeyman," author Stephen King. As befits a writer of horror novels in the modern Gothic tradition, King lives on a pleasant street of large, handsome homes in an oversized Victorian house reminiscent of the Addams family house, only without the cobwebs and rattling shutters. I won't reveal which home is his, but you'll likely be able to figure it out yourself. (Hint: If you spot a cast iron fence wrought with bats and demons, you're getting very close.) The house is on West Broadway between Union and Hammond streets. Take the Union Street exit on Route 95, travel toward downtown 6 blocks, then turn right onto West Broadway. (Don't confuse this street with Broadway on the east side of town.) But be aware that King lives in Bangor and not in Hollywood or New York for a good reason. Enjoy his home from a distance and please respect his privacy.

Orono and Old Town

About 8 miles north of Bangor in Orono is the principal campus of the University of Maine, with about 11,000 students. The university began in 1868 as the Maine State College of Agriculture and Mechanic Arts but broadened its curriculum over the years to encompass liberal arts as well as forestry, business, and engineering. The campus was originally designed by noted landscape architect Frederick Law Olmsted, but the plan was modified somewhat and later additions have obscured Olmsted's original vision. The campus, with its attractive buildings and leafy trees, still offers a pleasant place to stroll.

On campus you'll also find the **Hudson Museum,** a respected and well-designed museum of anthropology and native culture. Occupying three levels in a modern building with an open floor plan, the collections include gold and jade jewelry from the Aztec and Maya cultures of Central America and an exceptional selection of masks and carvings from the native cultures of the Pacific Northwest, including a towering and dramatic Haida house post. Other geographic areas represented include Oceania, the Arctic, and Africa, and there is a special emphasis on the native Penobscot Indians. Local crafts include cornhusk dolls, snowshoes, a birchbark canoe, ceremonial beadwork, and split-ash basketry.

The campus is located on Route 2A just off Route 2 in Orono. Check the campus map posted near the entrance for directions to museum. Open Tuesday through Friday 9:00 A.M. to 4:00 P.M.; Saturdays 9:00 A.M. to 3:00 P.M.; and Sundays 10:00 A.M. to 3:00 P.M. Closed Mondays and holidays. Admission is free. For more information call 581–1901.

Latter-day Penobscot and Passamaquoddy Indians still inhabit reservations around the state, remnants of early and inequitable land transactions between natives and settlers. One of the more prominent reservations is located just north of Old Town. **Indian Island** was part of a 1786 treaty that deeded most of Maine to the European settlers; the Penobscots retained ownership of more than one hundred islands in the Penobscot River, Indian Island among them. The island, which is home to the Penobscot Nation, is connected via a bridge to the west bank. Visitors are welcome with the understanding that the island is an active community and not a tourist attraction.

New prosperity arrived at the island in recent years following an $80 million settlement for outstanding land claims unearthed in early documents. The windfall has resulted in a handsome new school and the Sockalexis Memorial Ice Arena, named after the Sockalexis brothers, Andrew and Lewis, who went on to prominence in the Olympics and professional baseball earlier in this century. Skates may be rented at the arena (827–7776). Indian Island is also the site of high-stakes bingo games that aren't governed by the state (Indian Island is considered a sovereign nation) and consequently offer jackpots up to $25,000. The reservation usually holds two games per month; for a current schedule call 800–255–1293.

On a more poignant note, Indian Island also contains the gravesite of Joseph (Joe) Polis, a Penobscot Indian who served as Thoreau's guide and tutor during his travels through the forests of northern Maine. Polis taught Thoreau the Indian names for various flora and fauna, as well as the lore of the woods. As Thoreau noted, however, Joe wasn't entirely comfortable living off the land. "By George!" Thoreau quoted him as saying, "I shan't go into the woods without provision—hard bread, pork, etc." Their relationship is one of the more entertaining and interesting of the nineteenth-century literary world.

To find Polis's grave cross the bridge and drive a short distance to where the road forks at a cemetery. Park, then look for a granite stone topped with a small carved urn in the section of the cemetery closest to the bridge.

Old Town has become synonymous with canoes, thanks to the highly popular line of canoes manufactured by **Old Town Canoe Company.** The well-known company, founded by George Gray in his hardware store in 1900, is now the world's largest canoe manufacturer, selling about twenty-five thousand canoes a year—one of every four canoes sold in America. As a point of fact,

Old Town wasn't the first canoe maker hereabouts. That honor belongs to the White Canoe Company, founded in 1889, which was purchased by Old Town in 1984. Old Town phased out the White line in 1990.

Old Town still makes canoes the old-fashioned way, with wood strips and brass nails; but these canoes cost $2,500 and more, a far cry from the $40 they cost nearly a century ago. The more commonly purchased Old Town canoes these days are made of special plastics, Kevlar, and complex laminates, and by high-tech processes that would certainly confound Mr. Gray.

Despite the modern techniques employed, the factory is still located in a rambling brick and wood factory in downtown Old Town, with wide wooden floors and a healthy measure of time-worn corporate character. Inside the door and up a ramp, past several small displays about the history of the company, the Old Town factory showroom offers bruised new canoes at healthy savings over list price. A variety of other canoe accessories are also available here, from life jackets and repair parts to delicate Old Town ash paddles. The factory is an excellent stop for those truly intent on getting the most out of what Maine's North Woods has to offer.

The Old Town factory and shop is at 58 Middle Street, just up the hill from the municipal park. Open Monday through Friday 8:00 A.M. to 4:30 P.M.; Saturdays 9:00 A.M. to 3:00 P.M. Free half-hour tours of the factory are weekdays at 2:30 P.M. Call for more information, 827–5513.

Northern Penobscot County

From the Bangor-Old Town area, the county narrows and extends far northward. Settlements become more sparse, the lakes bigger and wilder. Many of the smaller roads turn to gravel with little warning. Summer communities thrive along some of the lakes, but for the most part the residents are year-round, and many find their livelihood in the forest as lumber workers or guides.

One of the less-known destinations for campers in the North Woods is the **Mattawamkeag Wilderness Park** just outside the small town of Mattawamkeag, north of Enfield on Route 2. The park isn't sparsely attended for lack of beauty; the place has a character that makes it seem like Baxter State Park's younger sibling. Relatively small at just over a thousand acres, this gem of a park sits alongside the wild Mattawamkeag River, a favored destination for serious white-water kayakers and fishermen. Smallmouth bass fishing is good in the spring, with Atlantic salmon arriving later. White-water enthusiasts are challenged by threatening rapids called The Heater and Upper Gordon Falls, both approaching Class V and portaged by all but the most experienced boaters. Those with less experience can enjoy some of the gentler white water above the falls. The park also features a network of hiking trails for exploring the riverside and flanking hills.

Mattawamkeag Park, owned and operated by the town, has nearly fifty drive-in campsites and eleven Adirondack-style shelters. Although it's called a wilderness park (some claim the forest has never been cut here), there are a fair number of amenities— hot showers, Ping-Pong tables, and horseshoes—that challenge even the most liberal definition of wilderness.

The park is an 8-mile dirt road drive east of Mattawamkeag, which consists of a couple of general stores, a laundromat, and a restaurant. The park is open May 15 to October 15. A moderate day use fee is charged; campsites are $8 to $10 per night. For more information call 736–4881.

It's hard to get a grasp of what life was like in the North Woods before the lumber roads changed the daily routine of loggers and lumber workers. The job is now much like any other: Workers commute to the woods from towns nearby, then return to hearth and home at night. Before the roads—and especially before the internal combustion engine—an entire subculture thrived in the forest as woodsmen spent weeks at their labors before venturing back into the civilized world.

One place to get a glimpse of that lost world is the **Lumberman's Museum** just west of the town of Patten. Extensive collections fill ten buildings, including one log cabin reconstructed from original 1860s loggers' cabins. This fine museum, housing thousands of North Woods artifacts, was founded in 1962 when the decline of the lumberman's culture was in the offing. Among the displays are early log haulers, a working sawmill, dioramas of the various types of logging camps that appeared in Maine, and literally hundreds of tools used by the loggers, millwrights, coopers, and others who depended on the forest for their livelihood. The reception center, housed in an old Maine Forest Service building, features evocative logging murals painted by local artists.

Open daily Memorial Day through September 9:00 A.M. to 4:00 P.M., except Sundays 11:00 A.M. to 4:00 P.M. Closed Mondays in June and September. Admission is $2 for adults and $1 for children under twelve. Located on Route 159 just west of Route 11 in Patten. Call 528–2650.

Continuing westward toward the mountains on Route 159, you'll cross the county line and come to the less-used northeast entrance to Baxter State Park, arguably Maine's most noteworthy outdoor destination.

PISCATAQUIS COUNTY

Piscataquis (pronounced Pis-CAT-a-kwiss) is the heart of Maine's timberland region and its least populated county. Even including the relatively populous towns of Dover-Foxcroft and Greenville, the county can muster only 18,000 residents, resulting in a population density of fewer than five people per square mile. Densely forested, the county is marked by attractive hills and beautiful lakes.

Baxter State Park and Vicinity

If you visited the state house in Augusta, you may have noticed in the rotunda the bronze bust of one of Maine's former governors. That was Percival Baxter, who served between 1920 and 1925. The reason he's been granted this place of honor is immediately evident when you're traveling in north-central Maine. Scan the horizon on a clear day and you're likely to see the distinctive sloping ridgeline of Mount Katahdin set amid the lesser peaks of **Baxter State Park,** Percival Baxter's gift to Maine.

Baxter, both as state legislator and as governor, attempted to have the state acquire the land surrounding Mount Katahdin. Displaying the traditional New England animosity to public land ownership, the state legislature rebuffed his efforts. Stymied but not defeated, Baxter set about purchasing the land on his own, using the considerable fortune acquired in part from his father, James Phinney Baxter, one of the pioneers in the Maine canning industry. Between 1930 and 1962 Percival Baxter bought bits and pieces and donated them to the state until he had assembled a block of land totaling slightly more than two hundred thousand acres. Baxter's central stipulation in handing the property over to the state was that it remain "forever wild."

The state has done an excellent job in carrying out Baxter's directive. The roads through the park are of dirt and often in rough condition. The number of campers allowed in at any one time is capped at seven hundred. And the 180 miles of foot trail throughout the park are maintained sparingly, making a hiking trip an adventure rather than a stroll. There have been some threats to the park's wildness: Literally hundreds of hikers now scale Mount Katahdin's 5,267-foot peak on a cloudless summer's day, overburdening the trails and compromising the wilderness experience on the summit. But dozens of other park destinations still offer visitors a place to be alone with the impressive silence of the woods.

Unlike most North Woods locations, Baxter State Park is a hiker's park first and foremost and a canoeist's park second. Day hikers will find a number of excellent destinations that are less daunting—and less crowded—than the Katahdin summit. Try the 2.5-mile round-trip hike to Big and Little Niagara Falls from Daicy Pond, or the 6-mile climb of Mount O-J-I west of Katahdin. The day use fee is $8 per vehicle per day (no charge for Maine residents). If you plan to camp at the park, reservations are virtually essential in the peak summer months. Baxter employs a pleasantly anachronistic method of accepting reservations: You must write in advance, requesting specific dates, and include payment with your request. Phone reservations are not accepted. Write for information on campsites and the reservation process: Baxter State Park Authority, 64 Balsam Drive, Millinocket, ME 04462. The most commonly used access point is the south gate, which may be reached from Millinocket along signed roads.

West and north of Baxter State Park are timberlands under the oversight of **North Maine Woods, Inc.,** a consortium of twenty-one landowners who banded together to manage recreational access. These companies and families jointly own and manage 2.8 million acres of woodlands, which are open to the public for a fee. Don't expect pristine forest, even though your road map may not show any roads hereabouts. As mentioned earlier, this is an industrial forest, managed for the production of fiber to supply paper mills. Recreational uses are secondary.

These woods hold few "destinations" for those who like their attractions neatly packaged. Access to the woods is on often dusty, unpaved logging roads, and you won't find much in the way of picnic areas or scenic turnouts. Along the way, drivers will see clear-cuts, regenerated forests, muskeg (a type of boggy ecosystem common in the northern woods), an occasional lakeshore, probably a roadside moose or two, and periodic glimpses of distant mountain ranges. Most recreation involves fishing, hunting, and canoeing. Because of state cutting regulations and the cooperation of the timber companies, most lake and river shores have remained unharvested for many years and offer a dense backdrop of mixed and softwood forests. When traveling by canoe, expect to see loon, beaver, and plenty of moose. North Maine Woods maintains about four hundred campsites, many of them accessible only by water.

Access fees are collected at various checkpoints around the perimeter. Maine residents pay $3 per day per person plus an additional $4 per person for camping. Out-of-state residents pay $6 per day plus $4 for camping. For a map and information, send $2 to: North Maine Woods, P.O. Box 421, Ashland, ME 04732.

Another way to take to the wilds is to sign up for a one-day rafting trip on the Penobscot or the Kennebec River. The West Branch of the Penobscot runs south of Baxter State Park and features one of Maine's most spectacular and demanding stretches of white water: a turbulent, rocky canyon called the Cribworks. After you maneuver through here, the remainder of the trip alternates between open river and quick, exciting plunges over short waterfalls and through narrow gorges. Exceptional views of Mount Katahdin open up along the way.

The early stretches of the Kennebec River (near The Forks in Somerset County) offer larger waves similar to those found in the canyons of the West, big enough to invoke genuine terror. The excitement runs its course fairly quickly, however, and you spend the rest of the day floating out of scenic Kennebec Gorge. Nearly twenty firms are licensed to run guided rafting trips on the two rivers. Their base camps tend to be concentrated near Millinocket and The Forks, and prices range from $60 to $100 per person for a one-day trip, which includes a riverside lunch. For a listing of white-water rafting companies, write Moosehead Lake Region Chamber of Commerce, Box 581, Greenville, ME 04441, or call 695–2821.

The region's early economic history isn't just a story of producing lumber. Well south of Baxter State Park is **Katahdin Iron**

Works, a state historic site that provides some insight into how iron was made during the mid-nineteenth century. Iron ore was first discovered by geographer Moses Greenleaf on Ore Mountain in 1843; within two years, Katahdin Iron Works was built near the site. At its peak in the 1870s and '80s, the works manufactured some 2,000 tons of raw iron a year, consuming upwards of 10,000 cords of wood to fire the blast furnace. A small village thrived here, with many of the 200 residents involved in hauling logs and producing charcoal in beehive kilns.

There's little trace of a village today at this remote site deep in the woods, but historical markers provide information about the iron-making process. Take time to marvel at two restored structures: the towering stone blast furnace with graceful arches at its base, and the massive brick beehive kiln (one of fourteen originally situated here) with its domed roof. The Iron Works are open May 20 to Labor Day. To find the iron works, drive 5 miles north of Brownville on Route 11, then turn left on a well-maintained dirt logging road, continuing on for 7 miles to a North Maine Woods gatehouse. The historic site is across from the gatehouse.

Eastern Moosehead Lake Area

The former frontier town of Greenville is located at the southern tip of Moosehead Lake, Maine's largest body of water. Lying at an elevation of just over 1,000 feet, Moosehead is some 32 miles long and ranges from 1 to 5 miles wide. With numerous bays and coves, the shoreline twists and turns for some 350 miles, serving as home to osprey, eagles, deer, and moose. There are a few vantage points here and there for those traveling by car, but for the most part you'll be required to travel by means other than automobile to get a good sense of the lake's beauty and drama.

One enjoyable option is to take a cruise on the **SS *Katahdin*,** a restored steamship (converted to diesel) that's been plying the waters of Moosehead since 1914. The *Kate*, as she's called locally, was built at Bath Iron Works and shipped in parts to Moosehead Lake, where she was assembled and launched by Coburn Steamboat Company. After a twenty-four-year career as a passenger ship, the 115-foot *Katahdin* was retired when the rise of the automobile made her economically unfeasible. She was then outfitted as a boom boat and used by lumber companies for hauling logs

SS *Katahdin*, Moosehead Lake

(towing logs encircled with a massive wooden boom) down the lake to the mills. The *Katahdin* participated in the state's last log drive, which took place in 1975.

To get a sense of *Kate*'s history, plan a visit to **Moosehead Marine Museum.** The museum owns and operates the ship and is located next to the dock in what passes for downtown Greenville. There's a small but fine collection of historical artifacts relating to Moosehead's history, including fascinating photos of the last log drive. Leave enough time to browse through the piles of scrapbooks, where you'll find insightful articles and mementos relating to the history of the lake, including pictures of the early fleet and menus from the original Kineo Mountain House.

The museum offers daily trips aboard the *Kate* throughout the summer. A two-and-a-half-hour cruise takes passengers up the lake past Moose Island and Burnt Jacket Point to the narrow pass between Sugar Island and Deer Island. This provides a good introduction to the size and wildness of the lake. A longer trip, offered twice a week, will take you halfway up the lake to Kineo Mountain, where you can disembark and explore the grounds of a once-venerable hotel. And for those who have an insatiable thirst for long boat trips, once a month the *Katahdin* cruises to the head of the lake at Seboomook, an eight-hour journey that provides a cormorant's-eye view of the lake's entire shoreline.

The *Katahdin* runs daily July through September and weekends Memorial Day through June. Prices range from $12 to $25 for adults, $6 to $13 for children. For more information call 695-2716.

For an eagle's-eye view of the Moosehead, several air services offer float plane trips from bases near Greenville. The planes fly high enough so you can appreciate the lake's size, but low enough to let you spot an occasional moose browsing in a marsh or along a river's edge. The oldest and best known is Folsom's Air Service (695-2821), which has been serving the North Woods since 1946. Although many of the once-remote lakes are now accessible by logging road, Folsom's offers quicker (and more comfortable) access to the entire region. Sightseeing flights may easily be arranged, ranging from a fifteen-minute tour of the southern end of the lake ($20 per person) to an hour-and-a-half-long fire patrol along the lake's full length ($35). You might also want to consider Folsom's fly-and-canoe package. They'll drop you and a canoe off at Penobscot Farm on the West Branch of the Penobscot River in the morning. After you spend the day paddling down the Penobscot and up gentle Lobster Stream, a pilot returns to pick you up at Lobster Lake late in the afternoon ($85 per person).

Even if you're not interested in a flight, it's worth stopping by the hangar at the edge of the lake, just north of town on Lily Bay Road, to soak up the atmosphere and watch the planes take off and land. For more information contact Folsom's. Other float plane charters serving the Moosehead Lake region include Currier's Flying Service (695-2778) and Jack's Flying Service (695-3020).

A wide range of accommodations is available in the Moosehead area, but two inns deserve special mention. The **Greenville Inn** (695-2206) is located on a hillside overlooking the village and the southern tip of the lake. Housed in an 1895 mansion built by lumber baron William Shaw, this fine inn is a virtual catalog of turn-of-the-century luxuries, ranging from marble showers to exceptional carved interiors of mahogany with cherry trim. The dining room serves excellent meals with popovers the size of footballs. The inn also has a comfortable front porch offering a view across the lake to the hills beyond. A room for two runs around $70, including a continental breakfast buffet.

Less luxurious and more remote is the **Chesuncook Lake House,** an uncommon inn accessible only by float plane from Greenville or by 18-mile shuttle boat trip from Chesuncook Dam. Operated since 1957 by Bert and Maggie McBurnie, the Lake House is situated on the wild shores of Chesuncook Lake with open views to the slopes of Mount Katahdin, 35 miles to the east. The inn, miles from the nearest road, is housed in a farmhouse built in 1864; gas lamps light the rooms and the delightful smell of Maggie's cooking often fills the house. Adjacent Chesuncook Village, once a bustling lumber town, now consists of a handful of summer cabins and a graceful white clapboard church. Thoreau stopped here on his way north in 1853 and visited the pioneer Ansel Smith, whose tombstone can be found in the cemetery next to the church. After exploring the old village on foot, rent a canoe from the McBurnies and set out across the lake to 3,000-acre Gero Island, where hay was once raised to feed the horses hauling felled trees in the vast forest.

Chesuncook Lake House is open year-round. (In winter the McBurnies move to a snug house a few hundred yards down the shore and rent out two nearby housekeeping cabins to snowmobilers and cross-country skiers.) Lodging costs around $70 per person, including all meals. Call 745–5330.

SOMERSET COUNTY

The west side of Moosehead Lake falls within Somerset County, which extends westward to the Canadian border. Like many of the northern counties, Somerset is long and narrow, encompassing a variety of terrain. This is also timber country: In every Somerset township from Bingham northward, timber companies own five thousand acres or more.

Western Moosehead Lake Area

The west side of Moosehead Lake between Greenville and Rockwood can be quickly covered on Route 15. The road is wide and fast, but it offers few glimpses of the lake until you approach the village of Rockwood. Here you'll be rewarded with a full view of what amounts to the lake's trademark: the sheer, flinty cliffs of Mount Kineo.

Mount Kineo has long been a landmark in the region. Indians traveled from afar to the cliff's base to gather its fine flint for weapons, and one Indian legend claims that the mountain is the remnants of a petrified moose sent by the Great Spirit as retribution for their sins. Late in the last century, the broad peninsula at the base was the site of the Kineo Mountain House, at its heyday perhaps the most grand of the Maine resorts. The stately gabled building boasted more than five hundred guest rooms, and the dining room could seat four hundred at a time. An immense annex was built to house the staff, some of whom tended a forty-acre garden to provide food for the table.

Alas, the Mountain House closed in 1934 and was demolished in 1938, after the automobile and the Great Depression sounded the death knell for the era of the grand resort. There is life arising from among the ashes today, however. Over the next couple of years, an ambitious investment group is planning to build a new resort community at the base of Kineo, constructing a fifty-nine-room inn out of the old annex (scheduled to open partially in 1993) and adding cluster-type vacation housing along the edge of the grounds. The golf course has been rebuilt and opened, and a small inn serves meals. Access is available from Rockwood via shuttleboat. The boat runs hourly and a nominal fee is charged. For information on the current status of the new hotel, call 534–2293.

Once at Kineo you can wander the grounds of the venerable resort and enjoy the extraordinary views down the lake. Be sure to leave two to three hours for the round-trip hike to Kineo's 1,800-foot summit. To find the trail, walk along the golf course, then cut across the eighth fairway to the old carriage road that runs along the west side of the mountain. Follow this about one-half mile to a rock with a white arrow pointing uphill. The steep ascent will take you along the cliff's face to a series of ledges looking southward toward Greenville. For a more expansive view, continue along the trail about another one-third mile to an abandoned fire tower, which may be ascended for a not-soon-forgotten view of the entire lake. (Not recommended for those afflicted with vertigo.)

The northern end of the lake at the village of Seboomook can be reached by logging roads in about an hour. The roads are maintained by Georgia-Pacific, which charges a day-use fee of $4 per car for Maine residents and $8 for out-of-staters. Like Kineo,

Seboomook during the glory days was the site of a fine resort, now long since lost. Remaining at Seboomook are a handful of summer cabins, a campground, and a small general store. Head into the store for an interesting sight: a collection of photographs of a World War II prisoner-of-war camp constructed here in the early 1940s to hold German prisoners captured in the African campaigns. Some two hundred and fifty prisoners were kept busy here cutting trees and hauling them with horses to the lake for the spring trip to the mills. Evidently the POWs, who were paid for their labor, were also treated well; many returned after the war to take jobs with the timber companies. Today, only the pictures remain. The buildings, including sentry towers and the ice house, have since been reclaimed by the forest and only an overgrown foundation or two may be found.

Route 201

A pleasant drive on Routes 6 and 15 will bring you to scenic Route 201 and the town of Jackman, the starting point of the Moose River canoe trip. This 34-mile trip attracts many canoeists throughout the year not only because of its scenic merits, but because of its convenience: Canoeists start and finish at the same point, linking the loop with a 1.25-mile-long portage between Attean and Holeb ponds. A couple of smaller portages around waterfalls are involved, but otherwise the river is gentle and forgiving, with only mildly challenging rapids. A number of riverside campsites are located along the way. Trip maps produced by the state are available at the several canoe rental shops in Jackman.

Heading south from Jackman along Route 201 will soon bring you to The Forks, where many of the rafting outfitters serving the Kennebec Gorge and the Penobscot maintain offices. (See page 135 for more information on rafting.) While you're at The Forks, a short side trip to dramatic **Moxie Falls** will prove rewarding. This beautiful cataract tumbles some 90 feet into a narrow slate gorge. There's a fine mix of forest trees hereabouts, with cedars and other softwoods mingling with birch. A trail skirts the gorge and offers good views of the falls. The brave and the foolish work their way down to swim in the turbulent, clear waters at the base of the cascades.

To find Moxie Falls, turn off Route 201 on the road along the east bank of the Kennebec River. (If you're coming from the south, that means turning right before crossing the bridge over the Kennebec.) Travel 2.7 miles and park near the sign indicating Moxie Falls. A trail of slightly less than 2 miles will take you to the falls.

Finally, before leaving the area, make a stop at the **Floodproof Wire Bridge** in the town of New Portland in the southwest corner of the county. This remarkable suspension bridge, built in 1841, has the aplomb and elegance of a miniature Brooklyn Bridge dropped in a wild, forested setting. The bridge's wooden deck is held aloft over the Carrabasset river on two thick cables made in Sheffield, England, rigged between two handsome shingled stanchions. The bridge was designed by F. B. Morse for the people of New Portland, who were weary of having their bridge wash out in the spring freshets. The fact that it still stands a century and a half later would suggest that Morse's design was successful. Indeed, in 1990, the bridge was proclaimed a Maine Historic Civil Engineering Landmark. To find this remarkable structure, turn from Route 127 onto Route 146 in the village of New Portland, then turn left at the sign indicating the way to the bridge. You can drive across through the polygonal openings, but really to appreciate the bridge, park at one end or the other and walk across. If you visit on a sultry day, there's a fine place to swim in the river just downstream.

Off the Beaten Path in The County

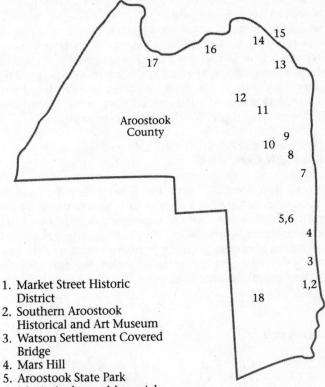

Aroostook County

14
15
16
13
17
12
11
10 9
8
7
5,6
4
3
1,2
18

1. Market Street Historic District
2. Southern Aroostook Historical and Art Museum
3. Watson Settlement Covered Bridge
4. Mars Hill
5. Aroostook State Park
6. Maxie Anderson Memorial Park
7. Fort Fairfield Blockhouse
8. Goughan's Strawberry Farm
9. Nylander Museum
10. Salmon Brook Museum
11. New Sweden Historical Society Museum
12. Stan's Grocery
13. Acadian Village
14. St. David Church and Tante Blanche Museum
15. Acadian Cross
16. Fort Kent Blockhouse
17. Allagash
18. Museum of Vintage Fashion

THE COUNTY

"The County"—as Aroostook is referred to throughout the state—has an uncommonly broad sweep and size for New England. Connecticut and Rhode Island together could fit inside it. Altogether, Aroostook County doesn't square with many preconceptions about Maine.

The gentle hills, broad vistas, and sprawling farmlands of the County share little with either Maine's sparkling coast or its dense North Woods. In fact, travelers would be forgiven for thinking they missed a turn somewhere and ended up in Wisconsin. They would also be excused for believing they've wandered into another era: Aroostook often seems to have more in common with the slow pace of the 1950s than the more hectic 1990s.

AROOSTOOK COUNTY

Most travel guides tend to ignore the County or gloss over the region in a page or two. Not only does it fail to resemble the Maine many travelers seek, but there are few tourist-oriented inns or restaurants. Don't let that deter you. The County has a subtle grandeur and fascinating immigrant history that reveals itself only to those who aren't too hurried to notice. For the inveterate explorer, Aroostook County is about as off the beaten path as Maine gets.

Houlton Area

Houlton, the county seat and oldest community in Aroostook, is a good jumping-off point for a ramble. Here the Maine Turnpike and Route 2 both come to an abrupt end and Route 1 passes directly through, suggesting Houlton's geographic importance. Despite its regional stature, this center of commerce has maintained a pleasantly drowsy character through the years.

Take some time to enjoy Houlton's **Market Street Historic District,** a block-long downtown showcasing a variety of commercial architectural styles from 1885 to 1910. Many of the fine brick buildings have happily avoided the depredations that befell other commercial districts around the nation in the name of modernization. Not that any of these buildings have been preserved as historical monuments. Houlton's downtown is strictly business as usual. There's a J. C. Penney, a video store, and a movie theater mixed in among the other shops. Look high along the rooflines at the intricate brickwork. Also be sure to note the elegant First National Bank building on the north side of the square, sandwiched between the theater and another bank. This small columned building dates from 1907 and is almost a caricature of the imposing banks that flourished at the turn of the century in many Eastern seaboard cities.

A short walk from Market Square is the White Memorial Building. This impressive 1903 Colonial Revival house, which lords over Main Street like a stern uncle, houses the chamber of commerce as well as the collections of the **Southern Aroostook Historical and Art Museum.** Items and artifacts of local industry and commerce are displayed in eight upstairs rooms, as well as in a downstairs room documenting Houlton's ill-fated Ricker College, which opened in 1848 and was auctioned after bankruptcy in 1979. Various historical items on display upstairs pique the imagination, including a dog mill to power a butter churn, badges from early Republican conventions, and a hand-carved wooden box filled with spruce gum (a typical gift of early woodsmen to their wives or sweethearts).

Keep an eye out for the elaborately detailed diorama of a man sitting near his canoe at a lakeside log cabin. Spruce trees line the forest behind him and a moose browses along the shoreline. What makes this notable is its construction entirely of matchsticks. In 1924 Leon Goodwin entered this work in a contest sponsored by a match company but was disqualified, since the contest rules required that whole matches be used. (Leon glued his into solid blocks, then carved them.) Contest judges were sufficiently impressed, however, to award Leon a special $50 second prize.

The museum (532–4216) is located at 109 Main Street and is open from early June to mid-September, Monday to Friday 11:00 A.M. to 4:00 P.M. Admission is free.

The **Watson Settlement Covered Bridge** is a short detour off Route 1 in Littleton, 5 miles north of Houlton. This bridge boasts two superlatives: It was the last covered bridge built in Maine (1911), and it's the state's northernmost covered bridge. Neither of these claims may seem particularly noteworthy, but the drive to the bridge through lush, rolling farmlands is a nice change of pace from the higher-speed travel on Route 1.

The 150-foot bridge isn't in use today (a more modern concrete bridge runs parallel to it), but visitors can cross by foot and sit along the banks of the Meduxnekeag River. A farmhouse and elms stand on the crest of a hill above, and songbirds proliferate along the banks, making this an inviting spot for a picnic. The bridge also has local distinction as a place for teens to express their affections for one another in ink and spray paint; there are some endearing sentiments emblazoned inside the bridge, and, of course, some not-so-endearing sentiments.

To get here turn east from Route 1 at Carson Road just north of the Candlelight Inn. (There's a small blue sign indicating a covered bridge, but it's easy to miss.) Drive 2 miles, then bear right down the hill where the road splits. The bridge is a few hundred yards beyond the fork.

Continuing north on Route 1, you'll soon see **Mars Hill** on the right, one of the few topological landmarks of any distinction in the County. This 1,660-foot-high mound played a cameo role early in the extended dispute between the British and the Americans over the border between the United States and Canada. Britain claimed this mound marked the highlands dividing the watersheds between the Gulfs of Maine and Saint Lawrence, the agreed-upon boundary in the Treaty of 1782. The United States disagreed and eventually prevailed on the issue of Mars Hill. The U.S. negotiators did, however, later concede extensive territory farther to the north in reaching a final settlement. Today Mars Hill is the site of a modest ski area on its west side and can be hiked for a bird's-eye view of the disputed terrain.

Presque Isle and Vicinity

For another high-altitude view of the region (or what passes for high-altitude hereabouts), head to **Aroostook State Park,** located south of the city of Presque Isle. The park—Maine's first state park—contains nearly six hundred forested acres situated between Echo Lake and Quaggy Joe Mountain. There's swimming and picnicking at the lake (which is ringed with summer homes), and camping at thirty sites managed by the state at the base of 1,213-foot Quaggy Joe. Hiking trails ascend both the north and south peaks, which are connected by a ridge trail, making for a 3-mile loop that can be hiked in a couple of hours. The north summit ledges offer fine views east into Canada as well as west across a blanket of dark forest extending to the craggy profile of Mount Katahdin. If time is short, bypass the south peak, which has limited views and an unattractive cluster of radio towers on the summit.

If you're wondering who Joe was and what made him so quaggy, you may be disappointed to learn that the name is merely a corruption of Quaquajo, the Indian name for the mountain. The commonly accepted translation is "Twin Peaked."

Aroostook State Park is open May 15 to October 15. Admission is $1.50 per person. Follow park signs from Spragueville Road 4 miles south of Presque Isle on Route 1. For more information call 768–8341.

Just beyond the state park on Spragueville Road is **Maxie Anderson Memorial Park,** marking the launch point of the *Double Eagle II,* the first hot-air balloon to cross the Atlantic Ocean. One early dawn in August 1978, Maxie Anderson, Ben Abruzzo, and Larry Newman lifted off in the glare of television lights from this farmer's field. Five days and 3,100 miles later, they landed unceremoniously in another farmer's field, in Miserey, France.

Their accomplishment was for balloonists the equivalent of locating the Holy Grail. Over the years dozens of people had attempted the crossing without success, and several had died in the process. To commemorate the historic event, a committee of Presque Isle citizens and businesses created a small park in the field with some modest landscaping, a pair of flagpoles, and a row of benches. The centerpiece is a 15-foot-high tin model of the *Double Eagle II* balloon and gondola mounted atop a brick and concrete pedestal. The park is dedicated to Maxie Anderson, who died in 1983.

In your travels through the County, you're bound to come across periodic references to the "Aroostook War" of 1839, certainly one of the more obscure and unremembered conflicts in American history. Hostilities—such as they were—were provoked by Canadian lumbermen venturing into territory that both the United States and England claimed as their own. The American government responded to this encroachment by sending thousands of troops to construct and man blockhouses in the Saint John and Aroostook river valleys. Emotions ran high, but reason prevailed before blood was spilled. After many tense months, the Webster-Ashburton Treaty of 1842 settled the boundary matter between the two nations once and for all.

A typical 1839 blockhouse may be viewed in the town of Fort Fairfield, just a musket shot from the present Canadian border. This replica was built in 1976 based on plans provided to the Maine Militia by Captain William P. Parrott. The **Fort Fairfield Blockhouse,** with its heavy timbers and overhanging second floor, was designed to withstand a formidable siege. Narrow windows, barely more than slits, allowed the militia to shoot out but weren't wide enough for bullets to enter by skill—only occasionally by chance. The overhang was created to allow the occupants to defend the main doorway and first floor by firing through openings in the floor. In the case of Aroostook's blockhouses, of course, all the planning was theoretical since no shots were fired.

Today the blockhouse is maintained by the Frontier Heritage Historical Society, which has filled the blockhouse with various and sundry items of local historical merit. These include a massive early wooden canoe, an old pedal organ, a wooden sheep catcher, and a "potato wheel" used to haul potatoes up from the cellar. The museum, located on Main Street across from the post office, is generally open daily July 4 to Labor Day noon to 5:00 P.M., but it wouldn't hurt to call the chamber of commerce (472–3802) to confirm hours.

If you're near Fort Fairfield in mid-July, plan to swing by for the week-long Potato Blossom Festival, which Fort Fairfield has celebrated annually since 1947. The festival lauds Aroostook's principal cash crop and includes road, river, and bike races; fireworks; a parade; and the crowning of the Maine Potato Blossom Queen. The festival is always held the third week in July and attracts upward of twenty thousand visitors from around the region. For more information contact the chamber of commerce at 472–3802.

Caribou and Environs

Driving on Route 161 from Fort Fairfield to Caribou, you'll pass by a rambling complex of farm buildings at **Goughan's Strawberry Farm.** This family farm is open to the public between May 1 and Christmas, with pick-your-own opportunities emerging up as each season unfolds. The farm is perhaps best known for its twenty acres of strawberries, which are open for picking for several weeks commencing at the end of June. There's also asparagus and rhubarb early in the spring; raspberries in July; and corn, pumpkins, squash, and gourds later in the fall. For visiting children the Goughans also maintain an animal barn with mountain sheep, turkeys, geese, pigs, and ponies. When in the hundred-year-old barn, be sure to notice the "ship's knees" construction—brackets hand carved from massive tree roots and used to hold the rafters in place. A small snack shop on the premises offers hot dogs, hamburgers, ice cream, and—what else?—strawberry sundaes and shortcake when berries are in season.

Goughan's is 4 miles east of Caribou on Route 161. To find out what's in season, call the recorded hotline at 498–6565.

Anyone with an interest in natural history would do well to visit the **Nylander Museum** in Caribou. This small city-owned museum houses the collections of Olaf Nylander, a Swedish-born amateur naturalist who was an inveterate collector of just about everything, but especially shells. Nylander came to Maine in 1880 at age sixteen. He earned his living as a housepainter, and spent his free time amassing vast collections of rocks, plants, and fossils from the local hills and forests, exchanging many specimens with scientists around the world. Much of what is known about the Devonian geologic period in Maine is due to Nylander, and several subspecies bear the name *nylanderi*. The museum, housed in a low building resembling a schoolhouse, was built to display Nylander's collections by WPA laborers in 1938–39. Nylander served as curator until his death in 1943.

The museum today still has an old-world feel to it, its extensive collections labeled in a tight cramped hand and displayed in old glass cases. Stuffed birds and mounted butterflies fill several cases (there's a wonderfully garish display of tropical birds), and Nylander's beloved mollusks are amply represented. A small gift shop offers field guides and other natural history items for sale; more serious naturalists can inquire about using the reference collection in the basement. Also take time to poke around the herb garden in the back, where you'll find eighty different species of medicinal and culinary herbs.

The Nylander Museum is at 393 Main Street in Caribou. Open Memorial Day to Labor Day Wednesday through Sunday 1:00 to 5:00 P.M. During the school year, open weekends 1:00 to 4:00 P.M. Admission is free. For more information call 493–4209.

If there's any one product that defines Aroostook County, it's the potato. The humble tuber has long been cultivated in Aroostook, and after World War I the industry boomed wildly. With prodding from Maine's Department of Agriculture, the production of certified seed potatoes grew from a mere hundred bushels in 1920 to more than five million bushels in 1942. Although the region's potato industry has been in decline since those golden days, about 90 percent of Maine's potato crop still comes from the County.

Given the central role of the potato, it's a bit disheartening to discover there's no potato museum anywhere in the state. One place that serves as a commendable substitute (until some visionary fills the gap) is the **Salmon Brook Museum** in Washburn, southwest of Caribou on Route 164. This sleepy town, home to a handful of general stores and cafes, can itself claim a place in the history of the potato: The frozen french fry was invented in Washburn and first manufactured by Taterstate Frozen Foods.

The Salmon Brook Museum is housed in an 1852 farmhouse in the center of the village, just off the town green. The simple but graceful home was purchased by the Salmon Brook Historical Society in 1985 and carefully restored to its earlier appearance. The ten rooms inside display nearly 3,000 items of historical interest, from a foot-powered dentist's drill to the town's original postmaster's desk. The displays are well presented and neatly organized, making Salmon Brook one of the better community museums in the state.

For exhibits related to the history of the potato, head upstairs at the agricultural museum in the barn behind the farmstead. You'll find a selection of turn-of-the-century potato harvesters and early potato planters, as well as several different versions of potato seed cutters and other agricultural implements. There's also a beautiful carpenter's chest from 1870 with a set of antique tools, and a circa 1950 chainsaw that appears as unwieldy as it does menacing.

The museum is open weekends from the end of June to Labor Day, 1:00 to 4:00 P.M., and by appointment. Admission is free, but donations are encouraged. For more information call 455-4339.

New Sweden and Vicinity

Northwest of Caribou along Route 161, signs of Swedish infiltration start to appear. You don't need to be an ethnologist to notice it: Towns like Jemtland, Stockholm, and New Sweden crop up along the way, and the mailboxes sport names like Sandstrom, Wedberg, and Johannson. On some homes you'll even notice painted detailing on the shutters reflecting the owners' Scandinavian heritage.

To learn more about how the Swedes came to settle the region, stop by the **New Sweden Historical Society Museum** in New Sweden. The museum is housed in a convincing replica of the community's early Kapitoleum, or meetinghouse (the original burned in 1971). Dominating the entrance is a bronze bust of William W. Thomas of Portland, who established the community in 1870. An American diplomat in Sweden under Abraham Lincoln, Thomas watched as thousands of Swedes packed off to the Great Plains and other points west to establish communities and build lives. Convinced that hard-working Swedes would contribute much to the state of Maine, Thomas persuaded the Maine state legislature to grant each willing Swedish immigrant one hundred acres of "rich and fertile soil." The first group, numbering fifty-one men, women, and children, arrived in New Sweden in July 1871.

The historical society's three-floor museum is filled with items from the settlement's early days, along with portraits of stern Swedish men and their dour wives. Among the more evocative items are an early bicycle with wooden rims, wooden skis (including one pair more than 9 feet long), a wreath made of human hair intricately woven and tied to resemble flowers—and a handsome tuba. Behind the Kapitoleum is the Lindsten Stuga, a typical early settler's cabin. This was moved from nearby Westmanland in 1982 and contains many of the original furnishings from the Lindsten family. Next door is a schoolhouse that the historical society plans to restore eventually, and beyond that the town cemetery where the local history is preserved in stone.

On the weekend closest to June 21, New Sweden celebrates the summer solstice with its annual Midsommar Festival. Each year hundreds attend this two-day pageant, which features costumed dancers, a maypole decorated with local wildflowers, and a festive procession to W. W. Thomas Memorial Park, located on a hilltop with endless views across rich, undulating countryside. At the park a distinctive wooden bandstand in a stately grove of trees is the focus of activities. The celebration ends with a folk dance in which the audience participates.

The Historical Society Museum is on Station Road just east of Route 161 and is open Memorial Day to Labor Day, Tuesday through Saturday 9:30 A.M. to 5:00 P.M., and Sunday 2:00 to 5:00 P.M. No admission is charged. For more information about the museum or pageant, call 896–3018.

Many in the local Swedish community maintain summer homes on nearby Madawaska Lake, just north of Jemtland on Route 161. And many of those summer residents make **Stan's Grocery** on the lake the destination for their daily stroll to catch up on local doings. A stop is worthwhile for ambience alone, even if you're not in the market for supplies. Housed in a building that appears to be fighting a losing battle with gravity, the store contains all variety of merchandise hanging from the rafters, and much of it has evidently spent more than a few seasons there. A handful of seats and a couple of booths overlooking the lake are arranged in an often-smoky room off the store, where you can enjoy one of Stan's ten-cent cups of coffee, unequivocally the best bargain in the state of Maine.

Acadian Maine

As you head toward the Canadian border, the Scandinavian influence fades and the Acadian presence grows. And grows. By the time you reach northernmost Maine between Van Buren and Madawaska, you're as likely to hear French spoken as English when you stop at a store or restaurant.

Maine's Acadians are descended from the early French settlers who made their home in French-ruled Nova Scotia in the seventeenth century. The British drove out the French in 1710 but allowed the Acadian settlers to remain. The two cultures got along on fairly good terms until the French and Indian Wars heated up in the mid-1700s. Fearing that the French-speaking settlers would support the enemy, the British dispersed the Acadians broadly to destinations including Louisiana ("Cajun" is a shortened slang version of "Acadian"), New Brunswick, and assorted other spots. New Brunswick initially welcomed the immigrants but eventually turned hostile and drove them to the Saint John River valley around 1785. The trials and tribulations of the Acadians were captured in verse by Portland poet Henry Wadsworth Longfellow in his epic poem *Evangeline.*

A good place for a crash course on Acadian culture is in Van Buren, home of the **Acadian Village,** or Village Acadien. This privately run museum consists of a dozen or so buildings, most of which were moved from other locations in the valley or are replicas of historic structures. Representative buildings span a broad time period, from the earliest days to the late nineteenth century. The structures are arranged in a field off Route 1 and include a shoe repair shop, an iron shop, a small railroad station, and a barber shop. (A visit to the barber shop might suggest how little the times have really changed.) The most interesting edifice is the Notre Dame de L'Assumption, a log-cabin chapel complete with a bell tower and a cross. Also on the grounds are a collection of baby carriages, an early post office, and the Emma LeVasseur Dubay Art Musuem.

The Acadian Village is open noon to 5:00 P.M. daily June 15 through Labor Day. Admission is $2.50 for adults and $1.25 for children. For more information call 868–2691.

Continuing north on Route 1, you'll soon hit the **St. David Church** and **Tante Blanche Museum** in the scarcely noticeable town of St. David (it's almost a suburb of Madawaska, a major mill town to the north). The Romanesque-style church dominates the countryside with its ornate brick facade and handsome stained glass windows, reflecting the strong presence of the Catholic church. The church building was begun in 1911, with the first mass held in 1913. Next door is the Tante Blanche Museum (open irregularly), housed in a small log cabin and named after an early Acadian heroine. The collections include an assortment of articles of early commerce, industry, and entertainment. Behind the house are an early schoolhouse and a nineteenth-century home representative of an Acadian settlement.

Follow the dirt road down the hill from the museum and toward the river. Shortly after you cross the railroad tracks, you'll arrive at the **Acadian Cross.** Erected in 1985 for the bicentennial of the arrival of the Acadians in the Saint John Valley, the cross is believed to mark the spot where the first settlers landed after descending the river by canoe. Also present are a series of seventeen memorial markers commemorating the original Saint John's Acadians.

Fort Kent Region

Another remnant of the Aroostook War (see page 147) may be found in Fort Kent, at the confluence of the Saint John and Fish rivers. The **Fort Kent Blockhouse** may look familiar; in fact, it's the same size and shape as the one described earlier in Fort Fairfield. But this isn't a replica. It's the real McCoy, constructed in 1839 by Maine militia dispatched to defend the frontier against British encroachments. Some ten thousand troops were stationed in the region for four years before the matter was finally resolved. The blockhouse, which is managed jointly by the state and a local Boy Scout troop, has a scattering of local artifacts dating from the Aroostook War era. A picnic area and tenting sites ($6 a night) are located along the Fish River adjacent to the blockhouse. Travel information is available in a nearby building.

The blockhouse is open daily 9:00 A.M. to 5:00 P.M. Memorial Day through Labor Day. For more information call 834–3866.

Blockhouse, Fort Kent

Near the international bridge crossing from Fort Kent to the Canadian town of Edmunston, look for the sign marking the end of U.S. Route 1. This meager sign seems a bit anticlimactic for the ending of one of America's more notable highways. On the other hand, the notice viewed from the northern side seems suitably humble and hopeful: "This marks the beginning of U.S. Route 1 ending in Key West, Florida, 2,209 miles south."

Following Route 161 westward from Fort Kent provides access to the northernmost timberlands managed by North Maine Woods, Inc. Through routes to other parts of Maine or into Canada are available only by way of roads that cross these private lands, and a sturdy, high-clearance vehicle is recommended. Those inclined to explore this interesting cul-de-sac without continuing onward can drive the 29 miles to **Allagash,** then back on the gently dipping and curving paved road. In midsummer you're likely to see a handful of vehicles with canoes on top pass you along the way. Allagash is the northern terminus of a popular 96-mile canoe route from Telos Lake in Piscataquis County. The drive is pleasant and pastoral, following a gentle river valley framed with fields that terminate abruptly at a forested edge. You'll pass several small villages along the way, each with a general store or two and little else.

French descendants predominate along the western river valley as they do to the east, but within this sea of French influence also exist descendants of Scottish settlers. There's little evidence of these contrasting cultures to the outside traveler, but the recent and well-received novels by author Cathie Pelletier (an Allagash native currently teaching at Vanderbilt University in Nashville) chronicle the picaresque adventures and misadventures of the Catholic and Protestant characters in the town of "Mattagash." The tales—included in *The Funeral Makers* and *Once Upon a Time on the Banks*—span several decades between the 1950s and the 1970s. Pelletier's books are available in a number of Maine bookstores; a third in the series, *The Weight of Winter*, was published in late 1991.

Route 11

South of Fort Kent Route 11 unspools endlessly through farmlands and dense forest. The road follows the route originally blazed hastily through woodlands in 1839 during the U.S. military buildup to defend the frontier at Fort Kent. The road's relatively ancient lineage is reflected in the surprisingly sheer climbs up hillsides that today would be leveled, blasted, and contoured by road engineers. The northern 37 miles between Fort Kent and Portage are designated as a Maine scenic highway, but the entire 98 miles between Fort Kent and Patten are as picturesque as you'll find anywhere in the state.

In Ashland make time to stop at the one of three restaurants—Chris's, Lil's, or the Four Seasons—for a slice of homemade pie. All three eateries quietly compete with one another for the loyalty of their patrons in a community that seems as if it could barely support one restaurant. As a result, the pies are remarkably tasty. The strawberry-rhubarb pie at Lil's, with its thick, crumbly crust and tangy filling, would almost be worth the drive from Kittery.

Few Mainers associate the County with fashion, but the exception is Francis Webb Stratton, founder and owner the the **Museum of Vintage Fashion** in Island Falls, about 10 miles east of Route 11. The fourteen rooms in this rambling old house contain some six thousand articles of clothing amassed over the years by Ms. Stratton, who's often on hand to lead tours through the museum herself. The collections are drawn primarily from the 1880s to the 1940s and include a 1907 mourning outfit, a 1927 Girl Scout outfit, and a 1940s leopard fur coat. Stratton has collected clothing more for love than for profit (she plans eventually to donate the building and her collections to the town) and is more than happy to reveal stories about each of the pieces displayed, such as a garnet velvet bodice worn to Teddy Roosevelt's inauguration.

On the third floor, be sure to ask about the 18-inch-high dolls made several years ago by a local artisan. The meticulously crafted doll clothing is intriguing, but even more interesting are the life-like hands and faces. According to Stratton, they're made from slices of Wonder bread soaked in Elmer's glue, then kneaded and sculpted. As they say in the real estate trade, must be seen.

Tours of the museum last about an hour and a half and cost $3 for adults, $2 for senior citizens, and $1 for children under twelve. The museum is open 10:00 A.M. to 4:00 P.M. in week-long spurts throughout the summer. The schedule varies from year to year. For more information call 862–3797.

Index

Index

Index

About the Author

Wayne Curtis is a freelance writer who traded the summers of Washington, D.C., for the winters of Maine in 1987. He's since explored the state by car, foot, canoe, mountain bike, ski, and sea kayak, the last of which he paddled 300 miles from Portland to Machias in the summer of 1989. A contributing editor at *Backpacker* magazine, Wayne also edits *American Hiker*, a magazine about trails published by the American Hiking Society. He's also written for *Down East, Casco Bay Weekly*, the *New York Times*, the *Philadelphia Inquirer, Yankee Traveler*, and *Outside* magazine, among others. Wayne lives on Peaks Island in Casco Bay.